DOUBLE BIND
**A Guide to Recovery and Relapse
Prevention for the
Chemically Dependent Sexual
Abuse Survivor**

DOUBLE BIND
A Guide to Recovery and Relapse Prevention for the Chemically Dependent Sexual Abuse Survivor

By Caryl Trotter

Foreword by Terence T. Gorski

Based on the CENAPS Model of Treatment

Herald House/Independence Press
Independence, Missouri

Copyright 1992
Caryl Trotter

Published by Herald House/Independence Press
3225 South Noland Road
P.O. Box 1770
Independence, MO   64055-0770
1-800-767-8181

Printed in the United States of America
ISBN 0-8309-0613-4

96 94   2 3 4

Contents

Foreword

The sexual abuse of children is a problem of epidemic proportions in this country. One out of three girls and one out of five boys will have an unwanted sexual experience before age 18. Sexual abuse is far more common among recovering chemically dependent people than in the general population. In the past the problem of childhood sexual trauma has largely been ignored. This has resulted in high rates of relapse. As the field has become aware of this "double bind," it has responded with techniques and methods that vary in effectiveness. Two major approaches have been used. The first is to ignore the problem for the first year of sobriety. The second is to do intensive experiential therapy immediately after the person becomes sober. Although these methods were helpful for some, they damaged others.

It became obvious to me that we needed a more systematic way to treat the chemically dependent sexual abuse survivor. So I began reading and attending conferences on the subject. In May 1988, at a conference in Albuquerque, New Mexico, I sat in on Caryl's workshop for adult survivors. I was impressed with her clear, practical model of sexual abuse recovery. Soon we began collaborating on applying her methods of treating sexual abuse survivors to chemically dependent people. The result was the creation of the Surviving to Thriving Continuum, a developmental model of recovery for the chemically dependent sexual abuse survivor. The model provides clear guidelines in how to integrate sexual abuse recovery issues with the developmental process of chemical dependency recovery.

I find Caryl's work to be concise and written in plain English, free of jargon. Her balanced methods of challenging thinking, managing emotions, and behavioral interventions are clincally sound. Recovering people can understand and identify with the various stages of recovery as well as the unique warning signs survivors show in their relapse process. I've received numerous reports from counselors that Caryl's methods are effective in reducing relapse rates among chemically dependent sexual abuse survivors.

I strongly recommend this book and its methods for chemical dependency counselors, recovering people, and their families. The information may save your sobriety.

Terence T. Gorski

Acknowledgments

I would like to acknowledge Terence T. Gorski for his collaborative efforts in creating the Surviving to Thriving Continuum. Were it not for Terry's interest in the field of recovery from sexual abuse and his belief in me, this book would not have been written. His phenomenal gift for conceptualizing, questioning, and eternal challenging have allowed me to mature as a therapist, author, and trainer. I am grateful.

I would also like to acknowledge Stefani Atwood, M.A., my business partner and undying co-therapist. Our work together for the past eight years has been deeply meaningful and productive. It's as if we have always known one another.

There are so many others who have shaped my work with adult survivors.: Jean Goodwin, M.D., for providing me with superior supervision, and Christine Courtois, M.D., for having written the first really clinical book on treating survivors. I still read her description of contact victimization. John Briere, M.D., for developing instruments which I have found so helpful. Ellen Bass and Laura Davis for writing books that really speak to the recovering survivor. Laurie Pearlman, Ph.D., and Lisa McCann, Ph.D., for developing a model of treatment for the resolution of psychological trauma that is understandable and clinically sound. And Judith Herman, M.D., for being the "grandmother" in the field of incest and sexual trauma.

I would also like to acknowledge my family—Russell, Ariane, and Katie—for putting up with my screeching over the computer and always smiling at me. Thanks guys.

To My Father

Introduction

Susan is a recovering alcoholic. She attends AA but keeps herself isolated and doesn't have much to do with other people. Her husband tries to help her get out of herself, but she resists his attempts and considers this nagging. He often feels she is "not there," even though she goes to work and keeps up the house. Their sexual relationship is at a standstill, and Susan is appearing increasingly depressed. She made one attempt to talk to her counselor about her problems but was told she wasn't supposed to get into heavy feelings until she had been sober for at least a year. Her husband is afraid she's going to start drinking again.

John has been in a chemical dependency outpatient treatment program for the past two months after an intervention by his boss and his wife. He was having trouble concentrating at work and was coming in later and later each day, or not showing up at all. He was frequently distant with his wife and children and increasingly snapped at them for the slightest thing. His wife attempted several times to talk to him about his behavior, but he insisted he was just going through some changes and that he would cut down his drinking. He revealed recently to his counselor that he had been molested by his brother as a child but that he had gotten over it. The counselor showed animated interest, defocused on his alcoholism treatment, and wanted to bring his brother into John's sessions so John could confront him. John felt terrified at this proposal and sorry he had ever brought it up. He dropped out of treatment and vowed he could stay sober without help.

Both Susan and John are survivors of childhood sexual abuse and are in a double bind. In Susan's case, her counselor believes in focusing only on her sobriety and fails to understand that Susan is beginning to have post traumatic stress symptoms resulting from her abusive childhood. In John's case, his counselor doesn't understand that John requires full attention to his early recovery tasks while being aware of the possibility that his abuse history may become a complicating factor. The counselor is overly involved in initiating intensive therapy and neglecting that John is likely to return to drinking if he defocuses on secondary issues. Both Susan and John are prime candidates for what's called "reciprocal relapse." That is the condition in dual diagnosis in which the symptoms of one disorder can trigger symptoms in the other and create the potential for relapse. Susan's post trauma symptoms are becoming acute and, if not managed, are likely to trigger cravings to drink. In John's case, should he proceed with the confrontation, he is likely to be overwhelmed and return to chemical use. Alcohol abuse by either Susan or John will impede their recovery process. Alcohol blocks their ability to feel the emotional pain necessary to motivate their work in counseling. Susan requires a dual focus on her post trauma symptoms and substance abuse. John primarily requires treatment for alcoholism while postponing any intense abuse work until his sobriety is stronger.

Professionals in the chemical dependency field are not well trained to identify and treat symptoms resulting from childhood sexual abuse. It has traditionally been held that the counseling focus for the newly recovering person should simply be staying sober in the first year and that no other issues should be addressed. Professionals in the mental health field are not well trained to identify chemical dependency and tend to view substance abuse as a symptom of underlying emotional problems. Consequently, many chemically dependent survivors of childhood sexual trauma are in a **double bind**. They begin having symptoms early in their recovery and are not given the validation and support they need. Or they are not adequately assessed for serious addiction. Overfocusing on either sobriety or secondary problems can create for the recovering person the potential for relapse.

Susan and John are survivors of childhood sexual abuse but haven't yet admitted it. They may seem fine to the people who know them, but inside they feel they are dying. Appearing normal and often quite functional, people like Susan and John feel ashamed, anxious, and afraid. Many survivors have no memory of having been abused and feel like they're going crazy. Others have some awareness of the abuse and are able to make some connection between present problems and their childhood histories. Either way, recovering from sexual abuse is a crucial task for increasing numbers of people. Because many sexually abusive families are also alcoholic families, the chances are good that those who are alcoholic and drug dependent will also have suffered abuse as a child. Studies have shown that from 10 to 50 percent of men who commit incest are alcoholic or psychologically dependent on alcohol (Crigler, 1984). If chemically dependent survivors are not given the opportunity to disclose their abusive experiences and receive validation crucial to healing, the stage is set for the urges and cravings to fuel a relapse episode.

This book is about recovering from sexual abuse. It is written for survivors who are aware of their abuse and for those who believe they may have been abused. It is written for those who chronically relapse when they encounter the strong emotions which coexist with remembering abuse. It is also written for counselors and others who are supporting chemically dependent people in their recovery. Considering the path of sexual abuse recovery can be frightening. Many survivors who begin their healing process get lost in the pain of remembering. But recovery *is* possible—from the first glimpses of memory to the full integration of the experience and moving on. The stress of recovering can create the urges and cravings which can fuel the relapse process. Understanding the necessary recovery tasks, typical stuck points, and predictable relapse warning signs can support the recovering survivor toward healthy, sober living.

Who Are the Survivors?

The breaking of family secrets often unlocks some of the major barriers in our recovery. Increasing numbers of people are disclosing how they were abused sexually, physically, emotionally, and spiritually. Each year the incidence gap between male and female survivors grows closer so that it's now believed that one-fourth to one-third of boys and girls are sexually abused before the age of eighteen by someone they trust (Russell, 1986). Many of these children learn quickly to use alcohol and drugs or compulsive behaviors to survive the feelings while being abused. A study of inpatients on a chemical dependency unit revealed that 74-77 percent of adult women admitted a history of childhood sexual abuse. Adolescent females reported a 71-90 percent rate of abuse, and 11-18 percent of male teens reported they had been sexually abused (Rohsenow, Corbett, Devine, 1988). Just as alcoholism is intergenerational, so does incest pass down through generations of families.

Survivors show unique patterns in their use of alcohol and drugs:

- Survivors tend to begin using earlier than children who are not abused (J. A. Kovach).
- Survivors use alcohol and drugs to enhance the emotional numbing necessary to survive while being abused (Courtois, 1988; Briere, 1989).
- Survivors use drugs and alcohol to provide psychological permission to express sexuality and rage (Courtois, 1988; Briere, 1989).
- While most children and teens use chemicals to get high, survivors use them to get by.

What is Sexual Abuse?

In order to recover from the effects of incest and sexual abuse, it is helpful to understand just what it is. The definition given by Incest Survivor's Anonymous, a Twelve Step approach to abuse recovery, serves as a comprehensive one. It is read in its totality at the beginning of each meeting:

From the viewpoint of the survivor encompassing the emotional, mental, spiritual and/or physical damage done to the child:

A betrayal of trust in overt and covert sexual contact or acts which possibly includes: Touching or non-touching, verbal seduction or abuse, and anal or vaginal intercourse. [Also] oral sex, sodomy, manual stimulation, and direct threats or implied threats. [Also] other forms of abuse between people who are related genetically, by marriage, or by living arrangements. [Also other forms of abuse by persons] in whom a child perceives a trusting relationship: i.e., mother, father, grandfather, grandmother, aunt, uncle, cousin, stepparents, or stepsiblings. [Also] included are a live-in or sleep-over lover, a brother, a sister, a neighbor, family friends, or a baby-sitter. [Also] anyone either known [to the child] or a stranger with a power advantage of any kind over the child. [Also] professionals such as a teacher, an extracurricular activities instructor, a coach, a professor, or a school principal. [Also a] nurse, a doctor, an orderly, a dentist, or a technician. [Also] a therapist, a social worker, a minister, a priest, or a nun. [Also] a shopkeeper, a landlord, a Scout leader, a laborer, or a janitor. [Also] an office worker, a pilot, U.S. military personnel, a lawyer, or a judge. [Also] a police officer, a mail carrier, a foster parent, a politician, a banker, a corporate executive or anyone whose employment or social standing puts them in a position of power over a child. This also includes any adult in a position of power who betrays the trust of a trusting adult.

When this trust between a child and an older child, sibling, parent-figure, or adult is violated, that act becomes incestuous. We put full responsibility on the initiator for whatever took place. The child's age may range from conception, newborn, preschool, school age, teenager, and older. Unfortunately, there are many ways a survivor can be victimized between conception and birth.

The last statement of this definition is intriguing, and prenatal abuse is something we rarely think about when we think of childhood trauma. I believe ISA is referring to the idea that the level of care of the unborn child can directly affect the child's quality of life once it is born. Such abuse can be inflicted in three ways:

1. The mother and fetus can suffer physical and emotional harm from domestic violence.

2. The child may be unwanted and the mother may attempt to terminate the pregnancy. Failing this, she may inflict emotional abuse by resenting or despising the unwanted child.

3. The mother may not want to be pregnant or cannot tolerate her changing body or life-style and inflict physical and emotional self-harm.

The resulting harm to the child is failure to thrive and lack of protection by mothers who are often untreated victims of abuse themselves. These children often suffer chronic victimization throughout their lifespan.

There is a continuum of sexual abuses which describe the different forms it can take—from seductive to the more violent. These include:

Seductive Abuse. This is a type of sexual abuse wherein the child or teenager is seduced by the perpetrator. Oftentimes these experiences are perceived as pleasurable, gentle, and nurturing, with the offender often giving the child gifts or special privileges. A client described to me how, as a child, she would visit her father on weekends and they would go into the city for a meal and entertainment. When she was 16 he secured an elegant hotel room and proceeded to seduce her. Until challenged in therapy, she had always remembered this as a special and nurturing time, neglecting that her father's behavior was completely inappropriate.

Covert Abuse. This type of abuse can also feel seductive but is more sexually overt in nature. It is often presented as accidental and entirely appropriate from the standpoint of the offender. This includes: sexual staring at body parts, in particular genitalia and breasts; violating privacy needs; and accidental touch which is sexual in nature. This also includes exposing the child to sexually explicit photographs, reading sexually graphic material to children, or telling sexual jokes. There are often suggestions of sex or "teachings" about sexuality which are voyeuristic rather than helpful.

Marie felt confused and uncomfortable about her father's behavior. When she would stay with him on the weekends he had a habit of lying on the couch after dinner and unbuckling his pants. A few times she noticed that his penis was exposed. He would often stare at her and make comments about how her breasts were developing so nicely and that she would someday make a boy so happy. Once he walked in on her in the bathroom and acted hurt when she told him to get out. She finally convinced her mother she wanted to be with her friends on the weekends and the visits stopped.

Overt Abuse. This type of abuse is the kind that we most often think of when we think of sexual abuse. It is any form of sexual abuse in which there is blatant sexual contact. This includes sexual touching, forced masturbation, oral-genital contact, sexual kissing, rape, digital penetration, or sexual hugging. It also includes using the child for pornography or in group sex.

Ritual Abuse, Torture, Satanic Abuse. These types of abuse, once thought rare, are now being revealed by its survivors in astonishing rates. This type of abuse is defined in the book *Michelle Remembers* as "a systematic series of emotional, physical and/or sexual abuses" (Smith, 1990). These are various types of rituals that may involve group sex, mock marriage ceremonies, forced ingestion of chemicals, and the mutilation and sacrifice of animals or humans. It may also include horrendous incidents of neglect where the child is tied on a bed for days, is left in closets, or is buried alive. Such experiences go far beyond issues of family betrayal and frequently create for the survivor serious adult pathology such as multiple personality disorder.

I had worked with Tony for several years before he began having severe nightmares of being covered with blood. He had had a premonitory sense for several weeks that he had killed someone. One afternoon he rushed into my office and told me he had remembered having been involved in some bizarre ritual wherein he was forced by several robed men to stab an infant in the stomach. Since that disclosure he has revealed increasingly horrific memories of dismemberment, murder, and even cannibalism.

The Bio-Psycho-Social Effects from Childhood Trauma

Whether the abuse was seductive but confusing, or violent and life-threatening, the aftereffects for the victim can be profound. Experiencing sexual abuse as a child creates problems in the physical, psychological, and social realms.

Physically: Victims suffer innumerable illnesses and disorders. Often the body remembers, creating for the survivor specific aches and pains which are direct manifestations of the abuse (i.e. pelvic pain). Survivors tend to dissociate or split off from their bodies. They neglect normal needs such as hunger, fatigue, and medical attention.

Psychologically: Children must utilize a wide range of coping strategies to deny, minimize, or otherwise make sense of the insanity of sexual abuse. The degree to which these defenses must be used can later create serious pathology such as chronic depression, dissociation (spacing out), and learned helplessness.

Socially: A child living in a family culture of lies which fosters incest must watch carefully for danger. People become suspect and trust becomes impossible. Adult survivors often find it difficult to be with people, or they have relationships that are abusive and neglectful.

Post Traumatic Stress Disorder

All survivors suffer some degree of post traumatic stress disorder (PTSD). This is a psychological disorder described in the *Diagnostic Statistical Manual,* a classification system which characterizes emotional problems used by mental health professionals. PTSD is described by:

1. Exposure to a psychologically distressing event that would evoke significant disturbance in almost anyone (i.e., earthquakes, war, witnessing a murder) *that is beyond the range of normal human endurance* [italics mine].

2. Later re-experiencing of the trauma in one's mind through recurrent dreams of the stress or through flashbacks.

3. Numbing of general responsiveness to, or the avoidance of, the external world, or loss of interest in daily events.

4. A wide variety of other reactions such as sleep disturbances, difficulty concentrating, memory problems, irrational guilt, and extreme alertness.

The severity of the symptoms of PTSD for survivors may be mild, moderate, or severe depending on whether they as a child were able to tell anyone and whether any degree of belief or rescue was offered. PTSD is also cyclical in nature, so that symptoms will swing from intrusive recollections to avoidance of memories or reminders of the trauma. This cycling allows the mind to be gently "dosed" with information that otherwise would be too overwhelming for the person. An important point is that PTSD symptoms are related *directly to the trauma.* Children aren't born with symptoms such as these and would not have the emotional disorder without having been exposed to abuse.

Wayne Kritsberg, in his book *The Adult Children of Alcoholics Syndrome*, refers to unresolved trauma symptoms as chronic shock. Quite simply chronic shock is the experiencing of a catastrophic event and not resolving the physical/psychological effects of that catastrophe. Growing up in an alcoholic or dysfunctional home can be a series of traumas/shock/repressions.

Chronic shock is made up of four stages:

1. Shock Event: An event that severely upset the child. This might include the death or imagined death of a parent, divorce, physical trauma, the death of a pet, and all kinds of child abuse including covert, emotional, and verbal abuse.

2. Shock Stage: The physical and emotional effects of trauma are felt. The body goes into gear for disaster—rapid heartbeat, breathing quickens, adrenaline rushes in, there is emotional shutdown, and there is a vacant look to the eyes. The child suffers disequilibrium.

3. Rebound Stage: The child makes immediate attempts at seeking original homeostasis. There is a need from the body to restore balance, the shutdown emotions emerge, and there is a strong need to talk about and express the feelings about the shock event.

4. Resolution Stage: The meaning of the trauma has been determined for the child. Feelings are released including fear, anger, terror, hurt, rage, and hopelessness. Equilibrium is restored and learning occurs from the event.

Unfortunately, in many alcoholic or dysfunctional homes such resolution never occurs.

Emily was five when her father asked her to take a drive with him in the country. Her father hadn't been around much during her younger years, so this was a very special invitation. She remembers that they sang songs and told silly stories on their way. As usual, her father brought along a cooler of beer. She remembers the rest of the story in bits and pieces. Being dragged through the pine trees—leaves sticking her in the back—some gooey stuff on her legs. She believes she passed out. When she came to, it was very dark and her father was lying completely still next to her. She was certain he was dead. She tried to rouse him—with no success. Several hours later he regained consciousness, they got into the car, and drove home.

Emily returned to her room and climbed into bed. Her overwhelming fear had turned to numbness. She had gone into shock based on the fear that her father was dead, that she was lost, and that something terribly bad had happened to her. For Emily this was a catastrophic event. The imagined death of her parent and intense fear of being lost threatened her physical and emotional well-being. With no explanation of the event she was left to make sense of it by herself. Children such as this learn to deal with the traumas of life in ways that help them survive, but this does nothing toward helping the child resolve the emotional effects of the trauma.

Responses to a child's trauma from a functional family include:

- The trauma is normalized. The child is reassured things like this could happen to anyone. It is not the child's fault.
- Emotional support is offered and the child is encouraged to discharge feelings.
- There is support from the community. The child is encouraged to speak with others.
- The shock is integrated.

Responses from an alcoholic or dysfunctional family include:

- Silence is the rule. The child must interpret the trauma as best he can, usually by blaming himself as this provides a greater sense of control.
- The emotions are not allowed expression within or outside of the family.
- The child shuts down emotionally to survive. The trauma becomes integrated into the personality structure.
- The memory of the trauma becomes disconnected from the self. It is forgotten or split off from feelings so that when it is recalled, it is done so with little emotion. A part of the child will remain in chronic shock until the original emotions are discharged.

Chapter 1

Assessing the Chemically Dependent Survivor

As we have seen, it is important to acknowledge that the *majority* of people seeking treatment for alcoholism and drug dependency have been sexually abused. Professionals in the chemical dependency field often don't recognize sexual abuse survivors or understand the role untreated post trauma issues can play in relapse. For some it may be ill-advised to begin addressing abuse issues early on in recovery. For others post trauma symptoms may begin appearing early, so that postponing sexual abuse recovery is not possible or clinically desirable. The damage inflicted by childhood sexual abuse is currently not being identified in treatment programs, resulting in increased relapse rates. There is a mistaken belief in traditional treatment that addressing abuse issues will deter recovery. The reality is that sometimes *not* addressing the issues will create the urgings and cravings that lead to relapse. What follows are three classifications of chemically dependent sexual abuse survivors that are designed to assist in separating out who to treat and when to begin.

Classifications of Chemically Dependent Sexual Abuse Survivors

As stated earlier, many survivors use drugs and alcohol for a variety of reasons. Many become addicted, some don't. Some require lengthy periods of sobriety before embarking upon recovery from childhood abuse; some are able to begin their abuse recovery early in sobriety. There are three classifications of chemically dependent survivors: (1) Active Addiction/Repressed Abuse Issues; (2) Active Addiction/Active Abuse Issues; and (3) Active Abuse Issues/Reactive Chemical Use.

1. Active Addiction/Repressed Abuse Issues. These survivors have the genetic predisposition to addiction. When they begin experimenting with chemicals they will show increasing tolerance over time plus physical withdrawal when the chemical is removed. With the chemicals requiring six to eighteen months to even clear the body, establishing sobriety must be the primary issue. Usually they show no active PTSD symptoms and often have no conscious memory of abuse. It is important not to go on a "witch hunt," such as suggesting to recovering persons that they may be undetected survivors and should begin working on constructing memories right away. Many will isolate themselves from the triggers which would activate memories, so that the relapse potential from abuse-related feelings is minimal. They tend to have childhood memories triggered as they progress into later stages of recovery, often after several years, and seek increased levels of intimacy.

Paul entered the addictive disease unit of a hospital to detox from alcohol and cocaine. He was at battle with his ex-wife for custody of their children because of his belief that she was neglecting them. He was also in some minor legal trouble. He believed his entrance into treatment would better his chances for custody.

Because he reported a lengthy history of incest as a child and outbursts of rage as an adult, his counselor referred him to the sexual abuse track in another part of the hospital. He had a few memories of the incest but had little or no emotion connected to his experiences. He reported his abuses as a "normal" course of his growing up and could make no connection between his current problems and his history of abuse. His main concern was that he stay sober so that he could keep his job and attain custody of his children.

2. *Active Addiction/Active Abuse Issues.* Like the first classification these survivors also have the genetic predisposition for addiction. They seek chemicals as self-medication for abuse-related symptoms. When the chemicals are removed from their system, the repressed emotions quickly surface, creating for the survivor a dual diagnosis of chemical dependency and post traumatic stress disorder. Both problems are treated simultaneously, as there is a high risk of relapse if the survivor is not offered healthy, sober ways of managing the PTSD symptoms.

Jason entered an inpatient treatment center for a 28-day program for his addiction to narcotics. About a week into his treatment he began having frightening nightmares and flashbacks of being sodomized as a young child. He would often cry out in the night and would refuse to sleep in his room without staff guarding the door.

Jason was provided treatment for his post trauma symptoms while he continued to work his early recovery tasks for his chemical addiction. He was given a strong aftercare program which included support for his addiction and his abuse issues and symptoms.

3. *Active Abuse Issues/Reactive Chemical Use.* These survivors react to the symptoms of having been abused by seeking self-medication through drugs and alcohol but do not become progressively addicted over time. By treating the

abuse-related symptomatology, the chemical use generally goes down. Abstinence is, however, strongly recommended.

Mary entered counseling to work on abuse issues related to her chronic feelings of low self-esteem, anxiety, and depression. She was assessed for substance abuse and was found to be drinking excessively to numb her pain and help her go to sleep.

Her counselor insisted she become abstinent, which was hard at first until she had other ways of managing her feelings. As she proceeded in therapy she thought less often about using alcohol to self-medicate and felt she was learning to deal directly with her post trauma symptoms and related abuse issues.

Sexual Abuse Assessment

All chemically dependent persons should be offered an assessment for the existence of abuse-related symptoms. They need to be helped in understanding that their current behavior is not "crazy" or "weird" but rather normal reactions to abnormal experiences. Also, by acknowledging the frequency with which abuse occurs some of the stigma is removed and adult survivors are given permission to address their issues as soon as they surface. This process is called **normalization.**

1. Active Addiction/Repressed Abuse Issues: This classification of alcoholic and drug dependent person can be given the "Forewarning Statement" early in treatment. This statement connects the sexual abuse as a potential for alcohol and drug relapse.

The "Abuse Symptoms Risk Scale" (see pages 30-32) should also be given to assess for abuse-related symptoms and their frequency. A scoring key is included which measures the survivor's risk for having mild, moderate, or serious post trauma symptoms. Results should be balanced with the recovering person's history and present problems.

Forewarning Statement

Many children raised in alcoholic or dysfunctional families are abused physically and sexually. Some people vividly remember this abuse while others have these memories totally blocked from their consciousness. Sometimes the memories and feelings from being abused return as you proceed in recovery and the "fog" of the chemicals no longer interferes with your thinking.

The following is a list of common symptoms associated with having been abused as a child.

- nightmares
- sexual problems
- panic attacks
- feeling unreal
- urges to hurt yourself
- sleep problems
- disturbing mental images
- fear of men or women
- memory problems
- suicidal thoughts or urges

If you begin to experience any of these symptoms, or others you feel may interfere with your recovery from chemical dependency, let your counselor know. If the symptoms are avoided they can create cravings and urges that increase your risk of relapse.

Abuse Symptoms Risk Scale

This exercise will help you determine if you may be at risk for having post trauma symptoms associated with being physically or sexually abused as a child. Such symptoms can complicate your recovery from chemical dependency and place you at risk for relapse. Your final score will generally indicate you are currently experiencing mild, moderate, or serious symptoms and therefore

- need counseling for unresolved abuse issues,
- can continue to focus primarily on your sobriety while keeping in mind your symptoms might become more noticeable over time and create the potential for relapse, or
- can focus solely on chemical dependency recovery tasks without great threat of abuse issues emerging.

Please check the symptoms which apply to you and how often they occur. The numbers that follow each of your answers should then be totaled for a final score. The scoring key is shown at the end of the exercise.

(Note: The following questions are among those most frequently associated with the clinical symtomology of post traumatic stress disorder in the intrusive phase. Answers are affected by many factors, including the presence of alcohol, drugs, or medical conditions. The scoring of this scale is designed to be used as part of a comprehensive assessment, not as a strict measurement instrument.)

1. Do you have nightmares?

[ ] Very often (4)
[ ] Often (3)
[ ] Sometimes (2)
[ ] Almost never (1)

2. Do you have difficulty enjoying sex or being sexually responsive?

[ ] Very often (4)

[ ] Often (3)

[ ] Sometimes (2)

[ ] Almost never (l)

3. Do you experience times when you become extremely frightened or panic?

[ ] Very often (4)

[ ] Often (3

[ ] Sometimes (2)

[ ] Almost never (l)

4. Do you have times when you feel disconnected or separated from reality or out of your body?

[ ] Very often (4)

[ ] Often (3)

[ ] Sometimes (2)

[ ] Almost never (l)

5. Do you ever feel the urge to hurt yourself?

[ ] Very often (4)

[ ] Often (3)

[ ] Sometimes (2)

[ ] Almost never (l)

6. Do you have difficulty in sleeping because you can't fall asleep, awaken many times, or wake up without feeling rested?

[ ] Very often (4)

[ ] Often (3)

[ ] Sometimes (2)

[ ] Almost never (l)

7. Do vivid, disturbing, confusing memories ever come to mind when you don't want them to?

[ ] Very often (4)

[ ] Often (3)

[ ] Sometimes (2)

[ ] Almost never (l)

8. Do you sometimes feel panicky for no apparent reason when you are around a certain type of man or woman?

[ ] Very often (4)

[ ] Often (3)

[ ] Sometimes (2)

[ ] Almost never (l)

9. Are there periods in your childhood that you can't remember for no apparent reason?

[ ] Very often (4)

[ ] Often (3)

[ ] Sometimes (2)

[ ] Almost never (l)

10. Have you thought of killing yourself?

[ ] Very often (4)

[ ] Often (3)

[ ] Sometimes (2)

[ ] Almost never (1)

Total Score: _____

l0-l5: Mild post trauma symptoms; primary focus is on sobriety tasks.

l6-25: Moderate post trauma symptoms; focus on sobriety tasks while learning to manage symptoms so they won't become a potential for relapse.

26-40: Serious symptoms. You need to be in counseling with someone trained in addressing both post trauma issues and relapse prevention.

2. Active Addiction/Active Abuse Issues: The dually diagnosed survivor should also be given the "Forewarning Statement" and the "Abuse Symptoms Risk Scale." This type of
survivor will likely begin presenting abuse-related symptoms
early on in treatment. They should be given a thorough sexual
abuse assessment which could include aftereffects checklists
and a family and incest history taken in a series of interviews.
Such checklists and interview formats are offered in the books
listed in the bibliography. Psychological testing might be
warranted if there is evidence of a personality disorder or
other serious pathology.

3. Active Abuse Issues/Reactive Chemical Use: This type
of survivor should receive a thorough sexual abuse assessment
including checklists, interviews, and psychological testing if
indicated. A drug and alcohol use questionnaire or interview
should also be given to address the possibility of active addiction. They should be told that continued use of drugs and/or
alcohol places them at high risk for becoming addicted and
that such use will only delay and complicate their recovery.

Approaches to Treatment

There are a variety of treatment settings that are helpful in
supporting the recovering persons depending upon which
classification of chemically dependent abuse survivor they
are and the severity of their abuse-related symptoms.

1. Active Addiction/Repressed Abuse Issues: Considering
that the major treatment task for this type of abuse survivor is
the establishment of sobriety, treatment approaches include
inpatient chemical dependency programs, outpatient programs,
individual and group psychotherapy, and AA and other
Twelve Step groups. The survivor is encouraged to seek
treatment for sexual abuse issues only when sobriety is well
established or when the abuse-related symptoms become severe enough to interfere with early CD recovery tasks.

2. Active Addiction/Active Abuse Issues: Recovering from

chemical dependency is the primary task for this type of survivor also. Yet the abuse-related symptoms can quickly challenge CD recovery tasks. Utilizing a dual diagnosis approach, the survivor may wish to seek treatment in inpatient or outpatient CD programs which are prepared to address both the chemical dependency and sexual abuse issues. Other helpful treatment modalities include individual and group psychotherapy, AA and Twelve Step groups, and sexual abuse support or therapy groups.

3. Active Abuse Issues/Reactive Chemical Use: Because survivors of this type drink or drug as self-medication for abuse-related symptoms and are not addicted to chemicals, the best treatment approach directly addresses the sexual abuse. They should be counseled as to their risk of addiction and their need for abstinence during the course of treatment. As mentioned earlier, continued use of chemicals places this type of survivor at high risk for developing addiction. Further, chemical use complicates treatment by slowing down the process not only of remembering and processing memories but interfering with the healthy management of feelings.

Carleen came into the hospital for acute post trauma symptoms including major depression, losses of time, and self-mutilation. She had been drinking heavily and smoking copious amounts of pot in an attempt to handle her overwhelming feelings of fear and rage. After a three-week stay, she discharged from the hospital into aftercare therapy. She continued to drink and smoke pot despite strong recommendations from her counselor not to. When she would have a particularly difficult session, she would use chemicals even more heavily. Consequently, she would stay in a fog much of the time, giving herself little opportunity to process and move beyond her memories. She was also unable to allow herself to finally release stores of anger or to find alternative ways to manage her fear. She continued to be depressed and have serious post trauma symptoms long after her hospitalization.

Treatment approaches include individual and group psychotherapy in which the counselors are trained specifically in incest therapy. AA and Twelve Step groups can be helpful if the addiction potential is high. Peer support groups can be immensely helpful such as Incest Survivors Anonymous and ritual abuse groups.

The following chart represents the three classifications of chemically dependent sexual abuse survivor and appropriate treatment methods:

Active Addiction Repressed Abuse	Active Addiction Active Abuse Memories	Active Abuse Issues Reactive Chemical Use
• Chemical addiction	• Chemical addiction	• Self-medicating use
• No abuse memories	• Active abuse memories	• Active abuse memories
• No PTSD symptoms	• Interfering PTSD	• Interfering PTSD
• Focus on sobriety	• Focus on sobriety	• Abstinence in treatment
• Defocus on abuse	• Focus on abuse	• Focus on abuse

Chapter 2

Recovering from Childhood Sexual Trauma

Many survivors ask: Will I ever get over this? How do I start? How do I know how far I've come or where I'm going? When survivors acknowledge they are having problems that interfere with their physical, psychological, and social lives and that these problems might be associated with dysfunctional childhood backgrounds, they have begun recovery. The process of recovery is developmental, progressing from basic to more complex tasks over time.

Successful recovery depends on completing tasks in order. Failure to complete earlier recovery tasks spells trouble for later, more complex tasks. A major error many survivors make is attempting more sophisticated tasks, like having a healthy sexual relationship, before they have acknowledged that sex has been difficult because of being sexually abused.

The Surviving to Thriving Continuum was developed to describe the developmental process of recovering from childhood sexual abuse. It can be directly integrated with the Developmental Model of Recovery from Chemical Dependency created by Terence T. Gorski. This model is described in detail in *Passages through Recovery: An Action Plan for Preventing Relapse* (Gorski, 1989). The continuum grid identifies common stuck points, reviews the relapse-prone and recovery-prone styles for coping with those stuck points, and reviews the predictable relapse process for survivors. This grid can help recovering survivors understand the recovery tasks facing them in the future and identify strengths and weaknesses in their current recovery program.

A strength in the continuum grid is the outline of recovery methods. Two mistakes have been made by the chemical dependency field in treating addicted sexual abuse survivors. The first was to avoid dealing with abuse issues for the first year of sobriety. The second mistake was to initiate intensive experiential therapy immediately after detox. Although these methods have been useful for some recovering people, they have damaged others.

The model which follows illustrates a balance of techniques designed to challenge victim thinking, learned helplessness, and other maladaptive cognitive processes developed during childhood and aimed at making sense of the insanity of abuse. The model also provides gentle and effective ways of managing the strong emotions which arise in moving through the recovery process. And lastly, the model encourages survivors to identify behaviors which no longer serve them and, in fact, might actually be placing them at continued risk for re-victimization.

Throughout the following discussion of the Surviving to Thriving Continuum you are encouraged to refer to the grid that appears in Appendix A. At the end of each stage we will return to Susan, whom you met at the beginning of the book, to track her recovery process.

Stage 1
TRAPPED
Transition

Let's return to the case of Susan. She is a 28-year-old alcoholic, married with two small children. She has been sober for nine months after having completed a traditional inpatient chemical dependency program. She now attends AA and individual counseling with a chemical dependency therapist. Her husband Dan attended family week while she was in treatment and has gone with her several times to her individual counselor. They have been focusing on the damage Susan's drinking has caused her family and marriage.

They are also beginning to focus on some of Dan's sexual concerns in the marriage. This increased focus on intimacy has created some symptoms in Susan which we read about early in the book:

- Susan is getting increasingly anxious and depressed.
- She is isolating herself from her friends and is avoiding Dan, particularly during those times when they could otherwise be close.
- She has been experiencing a repeating nightmare of being surrounded by men while she's in bed.
- She's finding herself confiding in her eight-year-old daughter.
- She often thinks of drinking as a way to escape her pain and to help her sleep through the night, not remembering the nightmare.

Susan is in the first phase of recovery called **trapped**. This is a pre-treatment stage when chemically dependent survivors are, at best, *simply surviving*. They are experiencing symptoms of overwhelming stress, and they are self-destructive or self-neglecting in their behavior. They believe they are able to control their chemical use but haven't yet entered treatment because they feel they don't need to. They are unable to have meaningful relationships with intimate partners or their children. Intrusive memories, images, and nightmares are a frequent occurrence. They can no longer count on their usual ways of coping and cannot accomplish the simplest tasks. At the end of this stage survivors have recognized the need for help; they accept that something is very wrong which they cannot manage alone anymore. They accept their chemical dependency and accept their powerlessness to control their use. To come to this recognition and acceptance most survivors experience the following:

1. Increased symptoms. The first element of the trapped period is when the survivor recognizes that her problems have become increasingly worse over time. Symptoms such as depression, panic attacks, and sleep disturbances which were once rare nuisances are now serious enough to disrupt her everyday life.

Using chemicals is one way survivors cope with feelings of shame and anger from being abused as a child, Once the survivor becomes addicted, new, more serious problems develop. As the underlying abuse-related issues press for recognition, the survivor copes through increased chemical use or other compulsive behaviors.

2. Family crisis. All families move through periods of difficulty, hopefully resulting in stronger relationships among all members. For the survivor, though, this is a time when family struggles become heightened with no relief in sight. There frequently are sexual battles, where the co-survivor(the survivor's spouse or partner) is desiring reasonable sexual intimacy and the survivor resists. This often leads to eventual threats of abandonment by the co-survivor, or the survivor threatens to leave if the need to control is great. Scared and feeling isolated, survivors may feel the impulse to cross over

The Recovery Process

Trapped	Hope	Reassessment	Integration	Validation	Emergence
Simply Surviving	**Stabilization**	**Early Recovery**	**Middle Recovery**	**Late Recovery**	**Growth/Development**
1. Increased symptoms	1. Recognizing self-destructiveness	1. Developing trust & self-awareness	1. Recognizing abusive family system	1. Confronting / separating	1. Daily confrontation of brainwashing
2. Family crisis	2. Managing shock & stress	2. Creating realistic "safety nets"	2. Reassigning responsibility	2. Expressing feelings appropriately	2. Identifying Trigger Symptom Cycle
3. Memory triggers	3. Acknowledging sexual abuse	3. Understanding abuse as root of symptoms	3. Grieving multiple losses	3. Developing a self	3. Healthy emotional expression
4. Developmental blocks	4. Recognizing chronic survival patterns	4. Catharisis of repressed memories / feelings	4. Examine support systems	4. Becoming a choice-maker	4. Creating a self-enhancing life-style
5. Failing coping mechanisms	5. Developing hope & motivation	5. Honor childhood survival strategies	5. Challenge learned helplessness	5. Establishing intimate relationships	5. Effectively managing life's transitions
					6. Expanding intimacy

Surviving → → → → → → **Thriving**

sexual boundaries with their own children, reenacting their own childhood abuse. Such abuse reenactments are common at this time, when situations occur in the survivor's current life that have a similar emotional meaning to the original trauma or dysfunctional family message of shame.

3. Memory triggers. Triggers are external stimuli such as a touch, smell, or a sound that create sensory reminders of the original trauma. Survivors are frequently triggered, unfortunately, during intimate contact so that they may "freak out" with their partner for seemingly no apparent reason. The body may remember trauma and act out with illness, aches, and unexplained pain or bleeding. Survivors may experience disturbing dreams, nightmares, or worse, begin having flashbacks. A flashback is a re-creation in the survivor's mind of the childhood trauma. A trigger may be difficult for survivors, but usually they can separate the past and present. In a flashback they are unsure if the abuse they're remembering isn't happening *right then.*

4. Developmental blocks. We grow from children to teens to adults by progressing through a series of developmental tasks (small children learn to crawl, stand, and then walk). Survivors typically live in families which are not supportive to normal growth and development so that as adults they are trying to accomplish very complex tasks without having mastered the simpler ones. One of these tasks is called **differentiation**, wherein the survivor has separated from the abusive family system and has developed a sense of *self.* Another developmental task is the healthy establishment of boundaries. These might be physical, sexual, emotional, or intellectual. Adult survivors have difficulty with enmeshed relationships, role reversals, and knowing what is appropriate developmentally in parenting their own children.

5. Failing coping mechanisms. As we learned earlier, survivors at this stage cannot count on their usual ways of coping; they cannot accomplish the simplest tasks. This is because their usual coping strategies have been "used up." What used to protect them from being abused or from feeling the effects of the abuse are now maladaptive. If isolating used to keep them safe from their perpetrator, it's that same isolation that keeps them from getting help now.

Using denial ("I wasn't abused")or minimization ("It was no big deal") is a common way to manage the effects of a chaotic family. Continuing to deny or minimize the abuse or its aftereffects keeps the survivor trapped in the hopelessness and helplessness of the past. Most abused children learn to dissociate, or emotionally separate from their experience in order to cope psychically. Adult survivors who continue to dissociate can be a danger to themselves, can isolate themselves from those who could help, and are not "present" for the internalization of recovery tasks.

Susan is depressed, isolating, and avoiding her husband Dan. She is having nightmares and breaking appropriate boundaries by confiding in her daughter. She reports these symptoms to her counselor in a session apart from Dan and receives validation that she is not going crazy.

Her counselor reminds her of an assessment for childhood abuse symptoms which she completed in treatment. Susan finds the form and notices that many of the symptoms listed describe her pretty well just now. Through gentle questioning by her counselor, Susan is supported in her need to explore the possibility that she may be having symptoms related to having been abused as a child. Susan is ready to enter into the second stage of treatment.

Stage II
HOPE
Stabilization

The second recovery phase is hope. The primary goal of this stage is to acknowledge the sexual abuse symptoms and manage/stabilize the acute stress which motivated the survivor toward recovery. It is a period of crisis intervention that may last many months for some. Memories of the abuse may be crashing in on the survivor, or memories may be vague and foreshadowing, a feeling that "something is about to happen."

Susan is given another assessment by her counselor that focuses on her family system, her history of abuse as a child, and any current aftereffects she perceives the abuse to have in her life now. Concrete intervention and stress-management techniques are offered, including increased contact with other survivors through a support group. It is in this group that she is given increased opportunity to talk about her abuse images and memories. Susan's counselor meets with Dan to describe PTSD, how it is affecting Susan, and the effect it is having on the marriage. The counselor suggests that they have no genital sexual contact for right now until Susan feels more in control of her post trauma symptoms.

A major part of this stage for Susan has been the reframing of her symptoms. Her depression is reframed as anger turned inward, the silence of abuse long held secret, and the recognition that the discovery of childhood abuse *is* depressing. Her isolation is reframed as a common coping mechanism of abused children trying to hide and feeling different from others so that they try to disappear. Her boundary violation with her daughter is reframed as a result of never having been shown healthy boundaries when she was growing up. Susan remembered her mother's complaints about unending sexual pressure from Susan's father. Her mother turned to Susan for solace and support, describing in detail his demands. Susan's urge to use chemicals was reframed as an understandable need for escape, for self-medication, and perhaps for punishment, as Susan clearly felt deep shame upon remembering her father's abuse.

1. Recognizing self-destructiveness. Growing up in an abusive family means being lied to. Children are told they are powerless, helpless, alone, and unworthy. Their basic needs are neglected and sometimes used against them to further the perpetrator's continued abuse. This kind of negative programming results in feelings of immense shame and worthlessness. Survivors may feel totally unlovable or that they are only good for one thing.

As a child, Larry came home abruptly from school each day fearing his mother's wrath if he was even one minute late. He was made to undress from his school uniform in the living room while his mother and sisters watched. He was allowed no privacy in bathroom activities and was told that holding his penis to urinate was "unclean." He was often forced to hold his urine for hours until told he could release it in view of others. He was sexually abused often through oral rape and forced masturbation by all three women and occasionally by his aunts. As an adult Larry often complained he felt like he was nothing, a "worthless piece of shit." His relationships were compulsively sexual, and he would sometimes seek several different partners in one evening. He was chronically depressed.

These internalized messages are at the core of survivors' self-concepts and are often acted upon in self-destructive behaviors. It is an important ongoing task to identify the offending messages that trigger the behaviors of self-destruction and design new intervening behaviors. Some of the more common self-destructive behaviors include self-mutilation (cutting), eating disorders, neglecting bodily needs, and chemi-

45

cal use. These behaviors often are fueled by thoughts such as "I hate myself," "I'm worthless," or "I'll never recover from this."

2. Managing shock and stress. Uncovering the reality of being abused as a child often is an immense shock to the system. Children *must* idolize their parents to assure their own worth and lovability. If the parents are abusive the child must create an image of the parents that continues to be good. Sometimes the child must even create delusions of these parents in order to survive. The shock which comes with remembering and acknowledging an abusive family system is enormous and can be emotionally debilitating. Stress must be reduced to a minimum, and the survivor's life-style must be examined and prioritized. It is not an uncommon response to "do more" in the face of increasing amounts of stress. Survivors deserve to be treated as if they had just been exposed to the original trauma.

3. Acknowledging the sexual abuse. Most survivors remember the abuse in layers, with the least traumatic memories emerging before more violent or distressing ones. At this stage it is important that the survivor begin to admit that there is at least a possibility of having been abused as a child. This may take the form of dreams, little flashes or glimpses, or through emotions or bodily sensations.

Trauma typically is resolved through a cyclic process of avoidance and intrusion wherein the victim cycles through denying exposure to any trauma and having intrusive images of that trauma. The survivor is encouraged to talk about what she is experiencing, be it vague sensations or flashbacks. This breaking of the secret releases energy necessary for coping with early recovery tasks.

4. Recognizing chronic survival patterns. We learned earlier that it is an ongoing process for the survivor to learn to recognize self-destructive thoughts and behaviors. It is the same with recognizing chronic survival patterns. This is sim-

46

ply honoring what extremes the abused child had to go to in order to survive. These patterns of survival take four forms: ways of thinking, feeling, acting, and relating to others.

Ways of thinking: These are the decisions the child had to make early on about his worth, his responsibility for the abuse, his helplessness, and his distrust of others.

Ways of feeling: These are the coping mechanisms the child used to psychically cope with the abuse such as going emotionally numb in the face of fear, anger, or sadness. Many abused children simply cut off their major needs (affection, attention needs) in order to survive.

Ways of acting: Children will act out in accordance with a combination of their belief system and repressed feelings. Some of these behaviors include isolating and self-destructiveness or seductive and promiscuous sexual behaviors.

Ways of relating to others: Some children cope by avoiding persons who resemble their perpetrators. Others bond with their offender, a common phenomenon between prisoners and guards in concentration camps. Such bonding can lead the adult child to seek other people and situations which remind them of the original abusive life-style and set them up for further victimization. Some have referred to this as a "trauma bond."

These survival patterns may have been adaptive as a child, becoming maladaptive symptoms as adults. Such patterns need to be assessed as to their current usefulness.

5. Developing hope and motivation. By now many survivors have begun to disclose some of their memories of abuse and have received validation and belief. They have talked to other survivors who are more advanced in their recovery and see that recovery is possible. By acknowledging the abuse there is a *reason* for feeling so bad. *The survivor discovers she is not crazy after all!* She readies herself to invest the time, energy, and resources necessary to recovery.

As Susan prepares to enter the next stage of recovery she completes numerous exercises and checklists. She goes over her sexual abuse assessment in depth with her counselor and lists current aftereffects which she can connect to her abuse history. She is utilizing the survivors in her group for support and is actively disclosing memories, images, and other awareness about herself to peers, her counselor, and Dan. She carefully monitors her stress level and has learned how to create "time-outs" for herself if she is becoming too overwhelmed. Although sometimes she has difficulty in believing her father sexually abused her, she is relying on the truth of her symptoms and the validation she receives from others.

Stage III
REASSESSMENT
Early Recovery

During this stage the survivor begins the process of internal change. In the stage of hope, there is an emerging awareness that there *is* a problem. In early recovery there is a reassessment of that problem, namely, the sexual abuse and its continuing effects on the recovering adult.

In the early periods of this stage the survivor is still having a difficult time believing the sexual abuse happened and fully recognizing its impact. By the end of this stage most will be able to appreciate how the abuse has affected them physically, psychologically, and socially. They will understand that the feelings of fear, anger, shame, and a host of other feelings are normal reactions to an abnormal situation and that they must be released in order to recover.

Through a series of writing exercises which she shares with her group members, Susan grows to accept her father's abuse of her. As feelings of intense shame and rage emerge, she reaches out to safe people and increases her sessions with her counselor. She makes the connection between survival strategies and her current symptoms. She discovers that her father would approach her sexually at night and would only touch her in a covert, seductive way. He would often stand over her bed for long periods of time before initiating the abuse. And sometimes he would simply turn around and walk away. Hence her dream of being surrounded by men while she was in bed began to make sense. This awareness caused intense anger, shame, and confusion. She never believed she had the right to complain because he wasn't hurting her physically. And besides, she knew she could never tell her mother who would never believe her.

Susan became quite depressed again and anxious over predictable future sexual encounters with Dan. Survival strategies which she discovered included her withdrawal and isolation from others, her avoidance of Dan and intimacy, going to bed early or staying up most of the night, overworking, and trying to keep up a good front. With these powerful pieces of information and insight, Susan moves into early recovery.

1. Develop trust and self-awareness. Survivors have survived by trusting few people and perhaps no one. They have been trained to deny everything they see, feel, and sense about their reality of the abuse so as to protect the perpetrator. In this stage the survivors are beginning to develop self-awareness through pairing their feelings and symptoms with their memories. For example, some may pair their chronic 2 a.m. awakening with the memory of having been abused at that hour. This task begins with a thorough assessment of childhood so that an intellectual understanding occurs toward explaining current problems. The emotional understanding or impact occurs later in recovery for many.

2. Create realistic "safety nets" (Atwood, 1988). As we have learned, remembering the abuse presents great shock and stress to the survivor's system. A solid support system is necessary for the recovering person's emotional security. Such people need to be safe; in other words, the survivor should be able to be completely honest with them, they should be able to be reasonably available to the survivor, and they should be tolerant that the survivor is likely to feel worse in recovery before she feels better. Safety nets should also include safe places (home, meetings, counselor's office, etc.) as well as safe "containers" of the traumatic images such as visualizations and affirmations. Lists are useful including who can be called or what can be done when the survivor feels scared, angry, or out of control. The survivor needs a lot of reassurance at this time when the feelings surrounding remembering may seem overwhelming.

3. Understand abuse as the root of symptoms. This is a task that goes deeper than the previously stated task of simply acknowledging the abuse, which is more of a "pre-awareness." This implies a deeper understanding that the abuse created few options for normal growth and development for the survivor. It is as important for survivors to acknowledge abuse as the root of their symptoms as it is for traumatized soldiers to recognize brutal combat as the root of theirs.

4. Catharsis of repressed memories and feelings. The survivor already may have begun the process of debriefing her abuse experiences without much emotion. During this stage feelings do begin to emerge, and the survivor may begin to dwell on the incest. Feelings of self-pity and periods of hysteria are common and are certainly understandable. The body may act out an abuse scene, which can be frightening to witness and more frightening to experience. Some survivors have few memories and will need months—if not years—before they remember. Memories are also selective in that they are not always perfectly accurate. Such accuracy is irrelevant at this time. The survivor's perception and psychic reality is the more important focus. It is important for counselors and support people to know that "abuse experiences should never be denied simply because they seem too horrible to have happened" (Ratner, 1990).

Jessie is a clear example of such emerging memory. He first sought treatment for depression in his early twenties. He was failing college, was severely depressed, and was having auditory hallucinations. He was quickly diagnosed schizophrenic and placed on high doses of anti-psychotics. He was in and out of state hospitals for the next twelve years. He would go for years with few or no symptoms, only to be followed by months of severe mental illness. During his "good" period he managed to get a degree in nursing.

When I began seeing him he appeared very psychotic and could do little but pound a mattress screaming "No—Stop!" In his more lucid moments he explained he felt like he'd been raped and was afraid to work with a male therapist.

Over the next three years I worked with Jessie uncovering what had happened. He had suffered numerous "hallucinations" such as the sense that blood was running down his throat. He also gave himself numerous enemas daily because he felt "dirty." Over time, through dream images, free association, journal writing, and art therapy, Jessie was able to remember horrific abuse experiences. He was abused as a very young child by several relatives, including his father. At age seven he remembered being taken to bars where his father was paid to have Jessie dance on the bar for an audience, not unlike a trained monkey. He later remembered that he would be sold off to the highest bidder at these bars where he would provide oral sex to the paying adult. This, Jessie believes, explains the "hallucination" of blood running down his throat. What else could a child have concluded?

In our last year of therapy he remembered being the star of child pornography, being sodomized by a gang, and witnessing the murder of a noncompliant child. The more Jessie became emotionally stable, the more violent the memories became. At first the memory images were fuzzy, came in bits and pieces, or appeared as "safe" people abusing him. These were terrifying to him as he thought it was just a matter of time before one of his caregivers would re-victimize him. Sometimes he would sit in my office and scream or cry, and I was not sure if he knew where he was. It was frightening for me at times. There were many memories that Jessie was unclear about, and he will never be able to "prove" them. But there were many he was *very* sure of which explained for him the bizarre symptoms that had landed him in state institutions. Today he is married, the doting parent of a baby boy, and completing his degree in psychology.

It is important to acknowledge there are reasons for defining types of memory recall. One is for clinical/recovery purposes, a subjective account. The other reason is for legal purposes, an objective account. In legal proceedings offenders can be held liable for a criminal act. So far in this book the references to memory work have been completely from the survivor's perception, with largely no need for objective "proof." When memories emerge or are reconstructed and processed for clinical purposes there is usually no liability issue. However, when children report sexual abuse proof is often needed so that necessary protection and care can be afforded the child. Children lie about being abused only about 5 percent of the time, usually because of a custody battle. In these the child has been coached to present an accusation against the parent fighting for custody. Recently several famous people have identified themselves as incest survivors in a public forum. Consequently, some of the families alleged to have committed these acts have sued for slander. Survivors need to understand the ramifications of publicly "speaking out" about their abusive experiences, which are often not received well by their families.

Another important point about doing memory work is that

there are at least four types of memory recollection. Unfortunately, human beings are not terribly accurate in their memory retention. Furthermore, when we are distressed we can sometimes confabulate memory to help us put meaning into an experience. A friend of mine shared with me years ago of having been abused by his father. He had little memory at the time. As he proceeded in therapy he believed he remembered his father hitting him over the head with an enormous piece of wood in front of six Boy Scout leaders who stood by and did nothing. Although this is certainly possible (you would think the Scout leaders would have to have been child abusers) my friend finally determined that this was fairly unlikely. Probably what truly happened was that he had been hit in the head at some time, perhaps by his father, but not in this public setting.

The four types of memory recall are:

- Those true memories which I remember accurately. I have always remembered it this way, and have many details. These are memories such as childhood games, school activities, or traumatic experiences which, for whatever reason, the survivor was able to integrate.

- Those memories which come to me through dreams, in "flashes," in bits and pieces, or in full images. These continue to build upon themselves until there is no doubt they are true. They begin vague and sometimes stay that way. They often make me feel crazy.

- I'm not sure of the memory and I have no way of knowing. I am doubtful. The evidence supports the memory only partly. They feel like several memories jumbled up.

- I have memories which simply do not fit what I know about the rest of my life. The evidence just doesn't fit my perception.

5. Honor childhood strategies. Most survivors don't know that abused children survive their trauma in fairly predictable ways. Helping adult victims to understand their coping behaviors within the context of survival mechanisms is an ongoing part of recovery. Behavioral aftereffects checklists are helpful at this time (Bass, 1989 & Blume, 1989). Some counselors find it helpful to talk directly to the adult's traumatized child-self. Sometimes the survivor feels there is a part of her who doesn't know she has grown up and is safe now. Some survivors find a childhood picture that triggers memories of how they acted as abused children. Even the most bizarre and shameful behaviors can usually be reframed as original coping mechanisms. As an example, many survivors admit to having perpetrated this themselves. This can be reframed as attempts at control and mimicking behaviors.

Judy almost always comes into my office, kicks off her shoes, curls up on the couch, and wraps up into herself. She has previously explained that as a child she would sit in her room for hours after her father had molested her and sit in such a way. I have learned to ask if "Little Judy" is here. When I almost always receive a quiet nod, I then settle into reminding this little one that she is safe, no one is going to harm her, and that she can talk to me. After a few minutes the "Big Judy" is free to come back and proceed with her therapy.

Let's return to Susan's recovery process. This early recovery period was a stormy one for Susan. She needed frequent reassurance that she was indeed sane and that she was at the "right place" in her recovery. Her counselor and group members would tell her, "You're right where you need to be." She spent several sessions with her counselor doing active rage work, including writing letters to herself as a younger, abused child. Susan once wrote a letter in her left hand as if she were that abused child writing to her adult self. The letter was startlingly sad and hopeless. As Susan proceeded with such deep emotional work she became aware of how she was part of a much larger system of abuse in her family. With this awareness she began to evaluate just how interactive she wanted to be with her family.

Stage IV
INTEGRATION
Middle Recovery

As they enter middle recovery, many survivors are regularly attending Twelve Step meetings and group or individual counseling. They have come to accept their victimization and have learned nondestructive ways of coping with the stress of remembering. They are coping more effectively in their day-to-day life but haven't yet achieved a balanced and satisfying life-style. The task of this stage is to complete a serious investigation into their abusive family system and to transform their victim identity to that of survivor identity. There comes a sense that the abuse was indeed real, that they were truly *not* responsible for it, and that changes are possible now because they are adults and have a good deal of control over what happens to them now. Specific recovery tasks are described below:

1. Recognizing the abusive family system. During middle recovery survivors may make major changes in their lives. They come to understand that incest occurs in a system within which the abuse is only a symptom. Understanding that sexual abuse doesn't occur in a vacuum, nor is it a rare, isolated event, helps survivors to know that they weren't isolated victims. There is initially an awareness of the mother's abject neglect of her child's abuse. There follows a harsher recognition of the possibility that the mother colluded or even participated in the sexual abuse. Occasionally survivors at this point will contact other siblings or family members seeking validation of their abuse memories. Sometimes other family members will also disclose their own abusive memories, further supporting the survivor's perceptions. Such contacts are encouraged only if the survivor is prepared for whatever response is offered, which can sometimes include blame and shaming from the family. Commitment to one's own reality and recov-

55

ery is essential before making this type of disclosure.

Maria thought she was the only one who had been abused by her brother. She began to research this by calling her closest sister and disclosing that she had been abused, was in treatment, and asking if the sister had also been abused. In a flood of tears of sadness and relief, her sister also disclosed similar abuse. Maria then called her three other sisters, and one of them disclosed abuse by this brother. The five sisters came together during a holiday and began comparing notes. It turned out that in Maria's family the sisters knew of many more cousins, nieces, and nephews who had been abused.

2. Reassign responsibility. Nearly every abused child believes that he or she is to blame for being abused. During this recovery task the adult survivor becomes very clear about who is to blame and reassigns that responsibility to the perpetrator and other accessory adults. This is often done in a concrete way such as writing undelivered letters, declarations in a therapeutic setting of the survivor's nonresponsibility, or talking to an empty chair where the perpetrator symbolically sits. Such reassignments reduce shame and guilt and allow understandable rage to come forth.

3. Grieving multiple losses. Abused children fail to grow and develop normally, so that they suffer basic losses of realities many of us take for granted. Survivors must grieve their lost childhoods, their loss of innocence, their loss of normal sexuality, and—one of the hardest—the loss of the hope that they will ever have a normal, nurturing family. Ratner (1990) describes grieving as a developmental process of accepting the reality of all the losses, experiencing or feeling the grief, and reinvesting the energy in new, healthy choices. Such grieving may feel and appear like the depression so common in early recovery. Survivors need to be reassured that the grieving process is one of moving forward toward resolution and in time they will integrate their losses.

4. Examine support system. The "safety nets" established earlier in recovery may no longer be fulfilling the survivor's needs. Middle recovery calls for the expansion of the current support system to include many people and places which provide for honest feedback. This requires examining the quality of the present network and seeking personal relationships that are meaningful and satisfying. Creating such relationships will take time and energy, and the survivor will need much reassurance and even skills training if he has little experience in making friends or reaching out. Supportive people can be found in therapeutic settings, at Twelve Step meetings, in spiritual communities, and sometimes in childhood families. Survivors are faced with recognizing their feelings, which leads them to their needs, then seeking out appropriate people in having those needs met. They also are challenged with learning to ask for and receive feedback for the purpose of applying new knowledge and taking new risks.

5. Challenging learned helplessness. The term "learned helplessness" was coined when attention came to the problem of battered wives. We now understand it to mean a certain way of behaving when one has been convinced by another that one is trapped. Numerous studies have shown that animals can easily be placed into the belief that they are helpless, so it is understandable that abused children learn early on that they too are helpless. Have you ever wondered why it is that a full-sized elephant doesn't simply pull the stake out of the ground onto which he is chained? Certainly it would take little energy to yank the post out of the earth. When domesticated baby elephants are being trained, they are chained and tied to trees for most of their young lives. As hard as they try the tree refuses to budge against their struggle. As the elephant grows up, he has long since given up pulling against his chain. He knows he is helpless and trapped. It takes nothing then to convince the elephant that the stump in the ground is the same as the original rooted tree.

During this time the adult challenges the victim identity and begins to envision a transformation to a survivor identity. As a victim you are helpless. As a survivor you have moved beyond being trapped. As an abused child there were no choices. As an adult survivor there is a new focus on autonomy and freedom. As the survivor begins to assert her newly discovered wants and needs, her family sometimes interprets this as "selfishness." Her assertions may in fact *be* selfish, as she can now ask for attention to her *self*, something that was never allowed in the abusive family.

As part of Susan's therapy she created an extensive genogram. On it she identified with the letters "SA" those people she either knew or suspected had been sexually abused. She marked "P" next to those she felt might be perpetrators. She also made marks for those she felt had problems with drugs or alcohol. She made calls to both her adult sisters, one who tearfully admitted to also having been molested by their father. Susan's older sister became hostile about her accusation, accusing Susan of bringing dirt into the family and wanting attention. She finally hung up on Susan. Susan, of course, became suspicious that this sister was also abused, but she decided not to focus on it at that point. Susan then set about writing a series of letters to her father which she never intended to mail. She read these to both her counselor and in her support group. In these letters she was very clear about what she remembers, that her father had no right to hurt her, what effects the abuse has over her now, and her reassignment of absolute responsibility to him for his actions.

This type of letting go prompted intense grieving for Susan, which she was afraid was her depression returning. At the suggestion of her peers, she began asking more directly to have her needs met. She would ask Dan to hold her if she was feeling scared. Or if she was feeling lonely she would call a friend and ask if she could spend the afternoon with her. Susan began to realize that she had been waiting for her family to change, namely that they would really show her how much they loved her. She was finally coming to terms with the fact that they probably weren't going to change and that she no longer had to feel resentful and helpless.

Stage V
VALIDATION
Late Recovery

The goal of late recovery is to resolve and separate from the victim life-style and create a new, healthy life-style based on the sense that the adult survivor is a whole person with a multitude of options available. The goal is not to forget the past but to integrate it and move beyond it knowing that healthy, positive relationships are possible. The survivor's new sense of self is validated in the choices made in her physical, emotional, and social realms. In order to attain these changes in life-style, survivors often move through the following tasks:

1. Confronting/separating from the abusive family system. Nearly all adult survivors feel the need to confront their perpetrators. This is most often accomplished symbolically, such as writing letters to the offender(s), acting out a confrontation in a therapeutic group setting, or completing a series of writing exercises such as those described in *The Courage to Heal* (Bass, 1989). Usually face-to-face confrontations are neither feasible nor safe. Most likely the offender will react toward the survivor much the same way he did when he was abusing her. When face-to-face confrontations do occur survivors generally want these things:

- They want the perpetrator to acknowledge his/her responsibility for the abuse and an explanation for the behavior.
- They want an apology and reassurance that the abuse has stopped.
- They often want the perpetrator to seek treatment.

- Sometimes survivors will request financial compensation for the cost of therapy.

Rarely do confrontations resolve with positive results. In fact, most involve the perpetrator continuing to offend the victim with denial, accusations of blame, or shaming; or blatant pleas of guilt followed by a "so-what" attitude. Survivors should never confront until they are prepared to defend themselves against any kind of response the perpetrator may give.

With the confrontation, whether symbolic or direct, comes a separation from the perpetrator and often from the abusive family system. This opens the way for the establishment of a new identity for the survivor.

2. Expressing feelings appropriately. Abusive families typically have a very limited range of expressed feelings. One family's main expressed feeling might be anger; in another it might be primarily sadness. These feelings are usually expressed with great intensity and often to the exclusion of other feelings. Children learn quickly which expressed feelings are acceptable and which will potentially make their situation worse. In this recovery task adults learn the language of feelings, the range of feelings, and expressed intensity. They also learn appropriate places and people with whom to express those feelings. Typical feelings which are discovered include:

- *Anger*: Learning to separate old anger from current and finding ways to put the feeling where it belongs. Survivors learn slowly to stop turning the anger inward, resulting in self-destructiveness and depression.
- *Guilt:* Often survivors feel unnecessarily guilty about their behavior as children. This needs to be challenged, reframed, and redirected.
- *Shame:* Sexual abuse is probably *the* most shaming of all offenses. Most of the shame adults carry is that which belongs to the perpetrators and must be reassigned.

- *Sadness:* The survivor must trust sadness in its expression to bring about emotional release.
- *Joy and Happiness:* Feelings few child victims ever know which must be consciously created as an adult.

3. Developing a "self." Most survivors don't have a clue as to what is "normal." They do know intimately what keeps others happy or what keeps them from being abandoned. Because there has been no support from a healthy family system for the abused child to develop as an independent, autonomous individual but rather someone who is going to take care of the adult's needs, the adult survivor now is faced with the serious task of self-discovery. It is the concrete answering of the question, Who Am I? It means examining personal tastes and styles, value systems, intellectual and leisure interests, physical and spiritual well-being, sexual preferences, and work-related and personal contributions and accomplishments. For many this means moving beyond the survivor identity, which can be as frightening as it is exciting. Many survivors make the mistake of choosing just the opposite pole of belief or behavior from that of their parent or perpetrator to find that their choice is equally dysfunctional! Such choices must be well thought-out and discussed openly with support people.

4. Becoming a choice-maker. This is a period when the survivor is putting into action the choices which were made in the section described above. It is the creation of a life plan that reflects a life-style based on healthy choices. Often there comes a sense during this time that the survivor must re-examine his spirituality. While many abusive families use religion to support and sanctify their behavior, other families simply provide no exposure at all to the concept of a higher power to their children. When adult survivors re-examine their spirituality, often they seek something greater than themselves and desire harmony and balance in their lives as it is expressed in nature. For many it is acknowledging Spirit in human form and the interconnectedness of everything. Many survivors have been severely spiritually abused, so that coming to this awareness may be slow for many and may not occur for some.

5. Establishing intimate relationships. By this time the adult survivor will have made many social contacts. Many of these will be acquaintances from meetings, workshops, and work-related activities. Some will be companions with whom the survivor shares common activities. Fewer will be true friends upon whom the survivor can emotionally depend and which will grow and deepen over time. If the survivor is in a committed relationship, this is the period when time and energy can be put into strengthening the partnership. One unfortunate outcome for co-survivors—the partners in love relationships with survivors—is that the relationship often takes on a lower priority during recovery. With little energy left to nurture a relationship, coupled with frequent sexual constraints placed by the survivor, relationships sometimes suffer tremendously.

It is important that co-survivors understand their partner's recovery process by reading, talking to their counselor, or attending support groups. It is critical for the co-survivor to recognize that once recovery has begun, the survivor may be making many changes, some of which many alter the balance in the relationship dramatically. Open communication, patience, and receiving support are important elements for any partner of a survivor in recovery. Friendships become more important, and the survivor must prioritize to make sure there is time allotted to see those important people. If the survivor has yet to become involved intimately with others, then she will need support and encouragement to do so now. To stay isolated is to continue in a victim life-style.

Susan has just come through a trying, yet moving period in her recovery. She initially planned a trip back to her hometown to confront her father face-to-face. She intended on demanding an apology from him and asking her mother where she was while the abuse was occuring. In preparation for this Susan practiced the confrontation with her counselor. During the session she became very frightened, regressed, and immobilized. Her counselor strongly encouraged her to back off the idea of a direct confrontation and to pursue it symbolically. Susan then proceeded to write caustic letters to both her father and her mother. She discovered she was actually angrier with her mother for her lack of protection than she was for her father's abuse of her. Susan read these letters to her support group and then burned them in a ceremony.

Susan did decide to send her parents a letter stating that she had remembered a number of things about her childhood which were causing her great distress. She asked them not to make contact with her until she had given them permission.

Susan was learning to identify and express her feelings. She was becoming increasingly verbal and assertive with Dan. One day she strolled into her counselor's office and announced that she had always wanted to go back to college but had never believed she was smart enough to make it. She announced proudly that she had enrolled for the spring semester.

Susan continues to carefully monitor her stress level, prioritizing her tasks and structuring her day according to how she is feeling. Dan and Susan have been working on communicating their wants and needs to each other, which has led them to greater comfort levels. They play together more and Susan has increasingly felt safer when she is sexual with Dan.

Susan has continued to attend AA this entire time and is maintaining sobriety. She now cuts back her counseling sessions to every other week. She is considering telling her support group that she will be leaving them to "go it on her own."

Stage VI
EMERGENCE
Maintenance

The last stage of recovery is emergence, where the focus of recovery is on the continuing growth and development of the adult's new sense of self. The goal is to acknowledge any residual effects of the abuse, confront them on a daily basis, and move beyond. This stage is never completed but is rather an ongoing process called productive living. The steps to take to accomplish this are:

1. Daily confrontation of brainwashing. Children learn self-concept by feedback from their parents and important others. If the feedback is positive and supportive, then the child will grow up with a healthy sense of self. Abusive families, however, tend only to mirror the child's feelings of worthlessness, stupidity, and unlovability. With these strong messages the child grows up with negative brainwashing. In this step adult survivors are encouraged to listen to the voices in their heads giving them self-derogatory and defeating statements, knowing that the origin of these judgments lies with the abusive family. These injunctions must be confronted as brainwashing and replaced with healthy, self-affirming statements. Oftentimes the brainwashing is subtle, and the survivor must rely on supportive others to listen for it and supply feedback.

2. Identifying the trigger-symptom cycle. We learned earlier that triggers are external sensory stimuli that cause the victim to reexperience the original trauma. In this step the survivor must discover what unique triggers are likely to cause symptoms or otherwise cause distress. These can be sought through the senses, such as certain smells, ways of touch, sounds or tones of voice, certain foods, tastes or tex-

64

tures, and anything viewed which could be triggering. Oftentimes there is not just one offending sensory trigger but an entire situation that presents itself as a trigger. The survivor's task is to identify as best as possible what triggers are difficult and either eliminate them as is feasible or integrate them by connecting them to the past and separating from that past.

3. Healthy expression of emotions. In earlier stages survivors have already learned what feelings are and have begun healthy emotional expression of a wide range of feelings. During this period they are expanding their communication skills and actively seeking places and people with whom to practice. They are taking responsibility for their feelings and setting boundaries with important others. They are asking that their needs be met and voicing their feelings about others' expectations that survivors meet others' needs. They express anger when it's appropriate and sadness when it comes up. They are able to walk through fear and identify what causes them to become anxious. The feelings which were once undifferentiated and stuffed are now named, experienced, and expressed in healthy ways.

4. Creating a self-enhancing life-style. Most people live their lives seeking truth and freedom of choice. Their choices will change over the years as their needs change. Survivors are no different. They are no longer chained to their pasts and are free to pursue a life-style based on what they want, what they need, and their new value system which has bypassed the survivor identity. They pursue a life-style that is a balance of physical, emotional, social, and spiritual support.

5. Effectively managing life's transitions. The nature of life is change, whether it is reflected in relationships, careers, and residences or in personal wants and needs. It has often been noted that people move through "seasons" just as in nature. There are gains and losses at each stage of maturity requiring for the survivor a graceful surrendering in the face of change. Where change would signify for the abused child a worsening of the situation, change now for the adult brings about new and positive experiences.

6. Expanding intimacy. The survivor's social system continues to develop with an emphasis on healthy expression of needs and wants. This period is when the survivor commits to recovering her sexual self. It is also a time when she may want to become involved with her community in particular groups which support other survivors or speak out on domestic violence. She may wish to become a sponsor or peer counselor for other victims. She understands that part of her total recovery is to share with others her courage, strength, and hope as well as the knowledge that adult children *can* recover from child sexual abuse.

Susan continues to do well. Her daily planning includes learning to listen for words that were brainwashed into her such as, "You're stupid" or "You'll never amount to anything." She is also learning to honor her unique triggers that cause her to lapse into old coping patterns. One trigger is simply going to bed. She has learned how to develop a bedtime ritual which includes a warm bath, talking with Dan in bed, and *then* negotiating about whether they are going to be sexual together. She has returned to school and is doing well. She continues to see her counselor about once a month but has stopped attending her support group. She still sees several of the women she met in the group but no longer is focusing on her incest. Her post trauma symptoms have all but disappeared, and she looks forward to a happy and successful life with her husband and children.

If you are a survivor, you may want to take a few moments to complete the Sexual Trauma Checklist found in the Appendix. It is a tool to help you assess where you are in the recovery process and to point out which recovery tasks lay ahead of you. As you go through each listed task, you will notice that you have already completed many but that progressively there are tasks which you have not yet accomplished. As you identify uncompleted tasks and have several in a row, you know fairly well just where you are on the path to recovery.

Chapter 3
Barriers to Recovery

Trouble Spots for Survivors

Recovery from sexual abuse is not a process of straight line growth. Most people recover in stages wherein they understand the dynamics of abuse, spend time applying and integrating this knowledge in their daily lives, then become comfortable and coast for awhile before the need arises for more knowledge. It is common for all survivors to backslide from time to time. This usually occurs when they are trying out new knowledge or challenging victim thinking and ways of acting. The stress of change causes them to back off for a while until there is time to reintegrate. This stop-start process is normal and to be expected.

Some people, however, don't make it through the recovery process, becoming stuck in the face of change. Because recovery is developmental, people achieve partial recovery when they hit a task that they believe to be insurmountable. When they fail to complete the task that faces them they become stuck. If they stay at this place they tend to fall back on old, maladaptive coping mechanisms, and sometimes serious trouble follows.

A productive response to hitting a trouble spot is to temporarily back off, talk with others about the difficulty of the particular task, and seek help in mastering the stuck point. If a stuck point is dealt with in an unproductive way, the relapse process can begin so that self-destructiveness and loss of control can quickly follow.

Successfully Coping:
The Recognition and Problem-solving Style

Survivors who are successful in moving through stuck points in their recovery tend to follow this process:

1. Recognizing the abuse as the cause of their symptoms and bad feelings.

2. Honoring their chronic defenses by understanding them as coping mechanisms used in childhood to survive.

3. Reassigning responsibility for the abuse to their perpetrators and others who failed to believe, protect, or rescue them.

4. Recognizing brainwashing instilled in them as a way to protect the abuser and secure the continuation of the abuse.

5. Debriefing their brainwashing by listening for it and replacing it with positive, self-affirming statements.

6. Taking baby steps in their sexual abuse recovery instead of giant steps before mastering less complex ones.

7. Trusting their process of recovery by learning from others who are further along in recovery.

Unsuccessfully Coping:
The Failure-to-Thrive Style

Many survivors unfortunately cope with their stuck points by denying they need help and then becoming focused on people and events outside of themselves. This process often takes the following course:

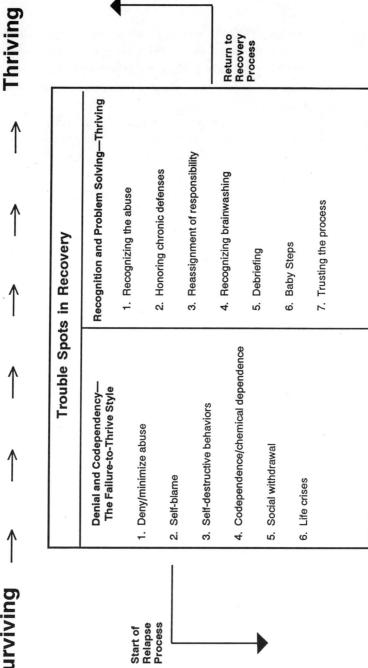

Surviving → → → → → **Thriving**

Trouble Spots in Recovery

**Denial and Codependency—
The Failure-to-Thrive Style**

1. Deny/minimize abuse

2. Self-blame

3. Self-destructive behaviors

4. Codependence/chemical dependence

5. Social withdrawal

6. Life crises

Recognition and Problem Solving—Thriving

1. Recognizing the abuse

2. Honoring chronic defenses

3. Reassignment of responsibility

4. Recognizing brainwashing

5. Debriefing

6. Baby Steps

7. Trusting the process

Start of
Relapse
Process

Return to
Recovery
Process

1. Denying and minimizing the abuse for its impact on the adult survivor. Other reasons are sought to explain that something is wrong, usually leading directly to self-blame. If the abuse cannot account for these bad feelings, then there must be something terribly wrong with them.

2. Self-blame is used to defend against growing feelings of helplessness but will further entrench the survivor in shame. This creates great stress which fuels the survivor to *do* something.

3. Self-destructive behaviors are a common outcome when survivors deny the abuse, blame themselves for their bad feelings, experience increasing levels of anxiety, and feel compelled to do anything for relief. Compulsive behaviors, such as overspending or acting out sexually, frequently do provide short-term relief but create worse problems later.

4. Codependence and chemical use often follow in attempts to manage feelings of shame and loss of control.

5. Social withdrawal follows as survivors fall back on childhood coping defenses and become silent. They withdraw from the very people who could help in challenging the stuck point and offering hope for reactivating the survivor's recovery process.

6. Life crises quickly follow, such as "re-victimizing" situations, serious depression, a suicide attempt, serious self-mutilation, abandoning important people, and dropping out of treatment.

Trouble Spots for Counselors and Caregivers

Recovering survivors are not the only ones who hit stuck points and need extra help in continuing on in the recovery process. There are certain survivor behaviors and issues unique to sexual abuse counseling that can be quite disarming for the counselor. Like the survivor, if the counselor can understand what her personal points of difficulty are, seek supervision and understanding, the counselor can probably continue to support the client in recovery. Denying that the counselor may be having trouble, having feelings of grandiosity, or being co-dependent with the client can actually *enable* the survivor's self-destructive behaviors, thereby leading to relapse. Let's review some of the more common trouble spots for counselors:

1. Dissociation continuum. We *all* dissociate from time to time, whether we take a five-second "staring into space" break or allow our minds to wander for long, elaborate daydreams. Dissociation gives us a mental break, necessary for psychic health and stress reduction. Survivors, however, don't just have pleasant daydreams. Abused children learn to dissociate themselves from what is happening to them, so they "space out" or become emotionally numb. Many children have out-of-body experiences and some develop other personalities to cope with the abuse.

Counselors may be uncomfortable or angry when their client dissociates during a session and fails to recall the session later. Dissociation is a particularly distressing phenomena when the counselor has worked hard on developing an intervention plan for self-destructive behavior, only to find out the client has hurt herself when in a dissociated state. Multiple personality disorder is being found to be less a rarity than once thought, presenting a treatment challenge few are trained for in traditional counselor training programs.

2. Severe post traumatic stress disorder. It is sometimes frightening for the counselor to witness the client suffering the severe symptoms of post traumatic stress disorder. As you may recall, these are symptoms of flashbacks, intrusive images, nightmares, and memory triggers. The particular difficulty of flashbacks is that it feels to the survivor that he is being abused again, *right then.* The counselor may find it difficult to convince the client that he is now safe, that no harm will come to him. Some survivors appear to "get stuck" in a flashback, so that no amount of reassurance can help the client to reorient to the present time. Counselors must understand PTSD, its manifestations, and know interventions that they can teach to their clients in an attempt to manage these potentially severe symptoms.

Jerry would sometimes go into a flashback while he was in group. It often would be triggered by his peers talking about their abuse experiences, particularly if the abuse involved groups of people. He would begin breathing heavily, his eyes would dilate, he would break into a sweat, and he would draw his arms and legs into himself. He would stare into space and appear "gone." Sometimes when I would ask him to tell me what was going on he would just continue to stare and tremble. Once I made the mistake of asking the person next to him to touch him on the shoulder which made him almost jump out of his chair. As a group we learned to honor Jerry's flashbacks and reassure him of where he was and his safety until he could finally hear us and return to the room.

3. Self-damaging behaviors. It is particularly distressing to witness a client who chronically engages in self-destructive behaviors. These include the multitude of behaviors designed to sabotage or defeat the therapy/recovery process: compulsive behaviors that become life-threatening; preoccupation with suicide; self-neglectful behaviors, particularly medical neglect; and a very trying experience, that of the survivor becoming aggressive toward family members, children, or family pets.

4. The discovery of ritual or cult abuse. This is difficult for many counselors to handle. Most are not trained in the treatment of victims of sexual abuse, much less counseling victims of torture and mind control. Therapists must be very clear as to their own tolerance level for disclosures of horrific violence and be willing to state this clearly to the client. For some this may mean saying up front that they are not prepared to treat this type of abuse and to screen out any potential client.

The difficulty with this is that so much of torturous abuse is not recalled until several years of therapy. Each counselor must make his or her own decision about referring a long-term client or staying with them and seeking supervision and training on this challenging issue.

5. *Countertransference reactions.* Transference is the projection of the client's feelings about significant others, usually parents, onto the counselor. Countertransference is the counselor's feelings and issues which are stirred by the client. Many counselors treating sexual abuse survivors experience "dread and horror" (Courtois, 1989) in listening to the violent accounts of childhood abuse. The counselor's worldview is challenged, and it is not uncommon to begin believing no child is safe, that everyone has been abused. Contact victimization is common, where counselors begin to experience their clients' symptoms. In an attempt to protect themselves, counselors might begin to avoid talking about the incest or denying its impact. Because recovery is fraught with relapses, counselors may begin feeling their counseling efforts are inconsequential.

6. *When to refer.* It is crucial to know what your limits are as a counselor and not attempt to provide treatment for something which feels over your head. Networking is an important element in this type of counseling, not only for peer support but to know who does provide treatment and what their particular approaches are. Counselors need to take responsibility for the need to refer and then be an active part of the referral process. Leaving the survivor to seek his or her own treatment after the referral often is interpreted as disinterest or, worse, disbelief in the survivor.

Chapter 4
The Relapse Process

The word "relapse" is commonly used to refer to those chemically dependent people who begin to use alcohol and drugs again after a period of sobriety. I suggest that although chemically dependent survivors certainly relapse in this way, they also relapse to former conditions of PTSD symptomatology, self-destructiveness, and victim life-styles after periods of more healthy living. There is a general comment that says if you're not recovering, you're relapsing. Recovery has also been likened to trying to walk up a down escalator. Recovery requires active, continuous movement upward. The bottom half of the Surviving to Thriving Continuum in Appendix A summarizes the common progression of warning signs that lead to relapse. You may want to review the grid now. For your convenience the relapse portion of the grid is duplicated on page 81. Not all survivors who relapse will experience all of these signs, but many will relate to these progressive symptoms of dysfunction.

The general course toward relapse is from denial of the abuse and its impact to self-neglect, coupled with an exacerbation of one or more high-risk factors. Then it only requires a minor trigger to set into motion the relapse process.

Most survivors come into treatment with certain high-risk factors which predispose them toward relapse. These factors don't *cause* relapse, they simply *increase the chances* that relapse will happen. High-risk factors cause survivors to be vulnerable to trigger events. A trigger event is something that occurs inside or outside the survivor which is a sensory reminder of the original trauma. Common trigger events include:

- symptoms of PTSD;
- reactions by others to the survivor's disclosure of abuse;
- re-victimizing encounters and situations such as contact with the offender or someone who resembles them;
- sexual encounters or medical procedures;
- real or perceived abandonment by important others;
- stress created by life's changes and choices that the survivor must make; and
- disclosures of abuse by family members, such as the survivor's siblings or their own children.

The relationship between the number of high-risk factors and the intensity of the trigger event determines whether the survivor will begin to malfunction. Survivors with few or no high-risk factors will require a greater stressor to trigger internal dysfunction; that is, changes in the way survivors think about things and manage their emotions. The opposite is also true. For those survivors with numerous high-risk factors, it will take only a minor trigger event to set off this internal dysfunction. Oftentimes internal relapse warning signs result from a buildup of symptoms which have become worse over time.

The symptoms of internal dysfunction are difficulty in

- thinking clearly;
- managing emotions;
- managing memories;
- sleeping or eating;
- coping with stress; and

• placing the responsibility for the abuse with the perpetrator.

The presence of these internal warning signs does not necessarily mean survivors will relapse. But such signs clearly set the stage for relapse if they are ignored, denied, or handled poorly.

As the internal dysfunction worsens, external problems begin to develop. Survivors who are fraught with internal difficulties find it difficult to function externally. An example of external dysfunction is those survivors whose anxiety has built to such high levels they have little control over their daily schedules. Unable to manage the anxiety effectively, survivors tend to *do more* in an effort to cope. Eventually problems erupt in their jobs, with their families and friends, and in their recovery programs.

Finally there comes a loss of control over judgment and behavior. Personal boundaries are lost and re-victimization is common. Survivors believe they have only three options: to self-medicate with alcohol and drugs, physical and/or emotional collapse, or suicide. Survivors of childhood sexual abuse have an eight times greater chance of attempting suicide than nonabused people (Courtois, 1988). With this loss of control comes deterioration, wherein the survivor is too malfunctioning to persist with recovery. Many survivors enter psychiatric hospitals or intensive inpatient treatment centers at this time. If help is not forthcoming, major pathology, divorce, chemical abuse, or suicide is possible.

Review the relapse grid that appears on page 81.

As we proceed through the relapse process we will follow John, the recovering person you met at the beginning of the book. As you recall, John began outpatient treatment two months previously due to an intervention by his wife and his boss. During one of his recent counseling sessions, he disclosed that as a child he had been molested by his older brother. The counselor had shown animated interest in this information and wanted the brother to come into a session so John could confront him. John denied that he had any feelings about the experience and had never even considered confronting his brother. After John's disclosure his counselor seemed less interested in his drinking problem and how it was affecting his work and marriage. John felt angry and confused. He dropped out of treatment thinking the counseling was useless. Now, with no support for his chemical addiction and his abuse disclosure left unprocessed and unsupported, John began to relapse. Let's look at how the process unfolds.

High-Risk Factors

Many recovering people come into treatment with strikes against them. These risk factors don't cause relapse. They just make it more likely that relapse will happen. Let's look at some of the more common factors for chemically dependent abuse survivors:

1. Severe post traumatic stress disorder. This is when the symptoms of post traumatic stress disorder are severe enough to cause major disruption in the survivor's everyday functioning. If survivors are dissociated and spaced out much of the day, appreciate how dangerous it is for them to drive, how disruptive it is to try to be in a relationship, and how nearly impossible it is to learn and apply recovery tools. Flashbacks can be immobilizing because the survivor feels the abuse is happening *right then.* The emotional effects and images from terrifying nightmares can linger into the next day, causing for the survivor anxiety and the inability to concentrate. Triggers seem to be everywhere, so the survivor may be tempted to isolate from people and places that could otherwise be helpful.

2. Torture/cults. The discovery of more severe abuse memories tends to take the victim to a different level of treatment needs. The return of these memories may shatter the survivor's belief system about family, justice, and the intrinsic

80

The Relapse Process

High Risk Factors	Trigger Events	Internal Dysfunction	External Dysfunction	Loss of Control	Deterioration
		Difficulty in . . .			
1. Severe PTSD	1. PTSD	1. Thinking clearly	1. Avoidance and symptomatic behaviors	1. Loss of boundaries	1. Suicide/homicide attempts
2. Torture / cults	2. Reactions to disclosures	2. Managing emotions	2. Crisis building	2. Poor judgment	2. Debilitating shame
3. Victim life-style	3. Re-victimization	3. Managing memories	3. Immobilization / depression	3. Inability to seek help	3. Abuse reenactment
4. Social isolation	4. Sexual encounters	4. Sleep and/or eating	4. Hypervigilance and anxiety	4. Acting on destructive impulses	4. Life-threatening problems
5. Self-neglect	5. Abandonment	5. Coping with stress	5. Social withdrawal	5. Option reduction	5. Substance abuse
6. Recanting	6. Changes and choices	6. Placement of responsibility	6. Confusion and overreaction	6. Emotional and/or physical collapse	6. Retreat into pathology
7. Flight into health/resistance	7. Other familial disclosures		7. Learned helplessness	7. Re-victimization and reenactment	

value of human life. The survivor may feel like she doesn't "fit" into those support groups which have heretofore been vital to her recovery. The process of memory retrieval may be immobilizing, and the therapeutic relationship can be strained or terminated. Most survivors don't acknowledge having been victimized through cults, but they may discover this high-risk factor much later in recovery.

3. Victim life-style. Children growing up in families who constantly victimize them find it difficult to attain a life-style with strong, independent boundaries. Many survivors come into treatment with life-styles that clearly resemble their original family dynamics. Family members continue to abuse and diminish the survivor, so that whatever recovery skills are learned in treatment are undone when the client goes home. The chronic victim reenactment blocks the survivor's ability to practice and integrate recovery tasks. Sometimes counselors must take an active stance in protecting the victimized client, such as insisting they go to a shelter, break off contact with offending family members, or limit the person's access to them (e.g., using an answering machine to screen all calls).

4. Social isolation. Many survivors come into counseling with few social contacts and fewer support people. Such isolation reenacts the original family dynamics by giving the adult no new frame of reference. It allows the internal voice of the perpetrator to grow loud, encouraging self-destructive thinking and behavior. Without others to engage in reality checks, the survivor falls into denial of the enormity of her problems and the adverse effects of the abuse.

5. Self-neglect. Abused children are neglected in the most profound way. Adults continue this legacy by neglecting their basic needs of eating, sleeping, and medical care. Such self-neglect leaves the body and mind unsupported in the energy required for recovering. Counselors must assess the adult carefully, collecting data on just how well the adult is caring for himself. This must be carefully communicated, for many survivors carry tremendous shame in the awareness that they haven't been taught the basics of caring for themselves. Sometimes it may be necessary to table abuse-related therapy until the adult is in better health, requiring referrals to doctors and other health professionals.

6. Recanting. This term means to withdraw something which has been previously declared. It is very common for abused children to disclose their secret to authorities and later recant. We know now this is due to the pressure the child receives from the offending family. Children are threatened with expulsion from the family or are told they will be blamed if Daddy goes to jail. The same is true when adult survivors recant. It is usually in response to having had contact with the family after a disclosure, and the internal or external pressure is so great the survivor takes back the disclosure. The need to stay attached to and protective of the family becomes more important than the survivor's recovery. This is best challenged gently in a peer group, for all know the temptation to recant with the hope of staying in the family and perhaps finally receiving the affection and attention they never got growing up.

7. Flight into health/resistance. Many survivors believe that once they have talked about having been abused that they are recovered and "fine now." We know that it is natural to believe that once the story is out, you should feel better. Unfortunately, any trauma is best processed by the telling and retelling of what happened. Although it usually doesn't take one's entire life to recover from abuse, it does take longer than a couple of weeks! This flight into health is usually simple resistance to going further into the recovery process which will likely bring about painful emotions. None of us wants to feel bad, and yet we know we have to feel the repressed feelings in order to recover from their negative effects.

The chronic buildup of stress created by these and other high-risk factors lowers the survivor's psychological and physical resistance. The more risk factors present, the less stress it takes to create internal dysfunction.

When John entered treatment he carried the high-risk factor of social isolation. John was raised a typical American male: to be strong, silent, and able to deal with whatever came his way. He had few friends, preferring to spend time at home with his wife and children. He rarely went out on the weekends, and when he was social it was always because his wife would initiate it. He was nervous and unsure of himself around other people, so usually he would make excuses to cut short his social time or get out of it altogether.

When John left treatment he had a second high-risk factor. He acted out a flight into health, telling his counselor that he had already dealt with the molesting by his brother. Although this might have been true, one wonders if, in fact, he did have great feelings of anger, confusion, and shame. The combination of social isolation and resistance to exploring abuse issues reenacts John's original family dynamics of silence and emotional numbing. He has no other frame of reference, such as other survivors, who could help to reduce the shame he feels. He has no one with whom to do reality checks. All he knows is that he is feeling worse about himself but has already made the decision to go it alone.

Trigger Events

Survivors have learned little in their childhoods about managing stress, so that as adults they typically respond to increasing levels of tension by doing more. Although their tolerance may be unbelievably high, most survivors at some point hit a limit and become dysfunctional. Usually what tips survivors over is the encounter with a trigger. A trigger is a situation that reminds them of the original abuse. Triggers seem to be everywhere, but there are seven listed below that tend to trigger internal dysfunction more than others.

1. PTSD. We have discussed post traumatic stress disorder and realize its potential to create chaos for the adult survivor. There are sensory reminders of the original abuse everywhere, including smells, tastes, images, a certain gesture, and voice tone. The list seems endless. Nevertheless, it is important to realize that for the survivor who is already under increasing amounts of stress, such triggers can create flashbacks and emotional re-experiencing of the childhood trauma which can be immobilizing.

2. Reactions to disclosures. A normal reaction to having been abused is the desire to tell someone. Most survivors do tell an intimate partner, friends, and sometimes family members from their childhood. Oftentimes such disclosures are met with support, understanding, and compassion, so that the relationship is enhanced. Other times, however, the survivor is met with blame and abandonment.

Spouses and lovers will voice revulsion, disbelief, and may express that they have been deceived ("You're not the person I thought I married"). Friends sometimes want to discount or minimize the survivor's story and want them to forget about what happened. Reactions from family-of-origin members tend to be mixed. Some tend to believe the survivor and go on to disclose their own memories of having been abused, and a new alliance is established.

More often the family becomes split, with much of the family loyalty remaining with the offender. The survivor is cast out as crazy and blamed for needlessly creating a scene. This can lead the survivor to recanting in order to hold onto the illusion of a family and look for other reasons to explain his symptoms. It can also create for the survivor deep mourning and loss, which must be expressed in order to move forward in recovery.

3. *Re-victimization.* Children growing up in alcoholic or dysfunctional homes are not taught how to establish appropriate physical, sexual, or emotional boundaries that will protect them. As adults, these children are unprepared to set boundaries and are often physically and sexually abused again. Such experiences usually trigger unrelenting shame and self-blame in the adult survivor. They may give up on recovery and use the re-victimization as "proof" that they are incapable of ever being anything other than someone else's victim. This is particularly stressful for the counselor who may be tempted to give up on the survivor, believing that the therapy is useless in the face of such victim programming. Understanding the inability of survivors to protect themselves is crucial at this time, as is direct counseling on assertiveness, appropriate establishment of boundaries, and perhaps a course in self-defense. The counselor is warned of the temptation to blame the victim, which must be challenged in supervision.

4. *Sexual encounters.* As the chemically dependent person moves into later stages of recovery it is normal to attain deeper levels of intimacy and a healthier sexual life-style than that before sobriety. It has been said that love brings up anything unlike itself, so that during intimate contact it is common for deep feelings to emerge. It is no different for adult survivors. Lovemaking can be triggering as survivors may suddenly feel their original perpetrator is once again committing incest. Flashbacks may occur or the lover may take on characteristics of the offender. If the childhood abuse was pleasurable, adult survivors may avoid sexual stimulation as a way to insulate themselves from the shame they feel. Some survivors seek sexual encounters as a way of self-fulfillment but feel great shame afterward if they are, in fact, re-victimized. Oral sex is an almost universal trigger for adult survivors. Counselors must respond to this trigger with understanding, couple counseling, and sex education.

5. Abandonment. Adult survivors are acutely aware that they may be difficult to be around. This high degree of sensitivity leads to chronic testing in relationships, frequent withdrawal, and acting-out. Abandoned as children, adults struggle with their own dependency needs while at the same time they try to avoid the devastation they feel if a relationship doesn't work out. Counselors are challenged to remain constant and consistent, helping the survivor express the losses left over from childhood. The counselor should be very direct in expressing his or her own limits and boundaries in regard to times available to the survivor as opposed to personal time. This is a particularly difficult trigger for survivors with borderline personality disorders.

6. Changes and choices. Something almost always happens in a child's family which activates the offender toward incest: his or her progressive chemical dependency; the physical or emotional abandonment of the spouse; or stereotypical role losses such as a job, the ending of an affair, or a demotion. Adults remember these family changes and, although they may not be able to articulate it, find change as an adult terrifying. Having no choices over any of the changes in childhood, they may reenact such helplessness as an adult. Change is a normal part of living, and survivors must be empowered in managing their lives now as adults.

7. Other familial disclosures. A particularly disturbing trigger likely to set off internal dysfunction in most survivors is the disclosure of sexual abuse by other family members. These may be siblings, cousins, or childhood buddies. More disturbing, however, is when the survivor's own children disclose that they have been abused, sometimes by the survivor's spouse or lover. This trigger can defocus survivors, sending them into a tailspin of a rescuing crisis. Strong intervention should be offered, including separating child and offender and strengthening the bond between the survivor and abused child. The adult's recovery should not be sidetracked but should be more closely monitored for indications that he or she is beginning to create justifications for self-destructive behavior or chemical use.

John continues to stay sober by attending AA several times a week. He has grown comfortable with a particular group and is occasionally speaking in meetings. If things could just continue this way John would be alright. He would continue to recover. However, at one meeting another man begins talking about how he was sexually abused as a child. He says he's been carrying this secret around with him for years and wants to get it off his chest. He goes on to describe how he too was molested by an older brother who was violent with him and sometimes brought in his friends to watch or participate.

John becomes triggered. He returns home after the meeting silent. He stays up the night thinking about his own childhood experience. Because the man at the meeting also disclosed that he is gay, John begins doubting his own masculinity. He wonders if he did something to provoke his brother. He fears he may have homosexual tendencies. He begins doubting his worth as a husband, father, and man.

Internal Dysfunction

Experiencing any one of the above triggers can cause severe stress. Not managing the stress, which is so typical for survivors, can lead to difficulty in thinking clearly, managing feelings and memories, and physical problems. The symptoms of internal dysfunction can be frightening, and many people believe they are going crazy. Let's review some of them:

1. Difficulty in thinking clearly. One very typical way abused children survive is by dissociating from their experience. Adult survivors often have trouble thinking clearly or solving simple problems because they are "not here." At times they are obsessing on the incest or a trigger event. Other times they are shut down and purposely avoiding stimulation. I've often likened this to feeling like there are too many plugs going into one socket: overload followed by blowout. Concentration is impaired and logical thinking is difficult to maintain for longer than a few minutes. Consequently, survivors cannot make one thought relate to the next and feel they cannot trust themselves or their judgment. The role of food and sleep deprivation should not be overlooked as a possible explanation for impaired thinking. Survivors will often fail to eat or sleep as a response to stress or during intense memory recall.

  2. Difficulty in managing emotions. Most survivors have what has been called an "incest filter," which is a way of thinking about everything as it relates to decisions the abused child made at the time of the abuse. As a result, survivors overreact to situations and people, or misjudge them. There is little room for reality testing because everyone and everything becomes aligned with their experience as a victimized child. Sometimes survivors feel nothing or are unable to know what they are feeling. At other times they are overwhelmed with feeling but cannot attach it to anything, so they feel crazy. Deepening depression, panic attacks, free-floating anxiety, and fear are common. Not trusting their emotions, survivors may attempt to ignore, deny, or stuff them. Or the feelings may come out "sideways" through the inappropriate expression of anger and violence or through compulsive behaviors.

  3. Difficulty in managing memories. Many survivors repress or block their abuse memories and may have lost years of their childhoods. As these memories begin to return, they may become all intrusive. Such intrusive images may kick off for the survivor original thoughts, feelings, and behaviors of a helpless child. Survivors in recovery may find it difficult to contain these memories and they may tend to spill over into work and family life. Furthermore, survivors find it difficult to remember current tools necessary in their recovery. In other words, they remember what they'd like to forget and forget what they need to remember! Some survivors get stuck in the quest for more and more memories as validation of their survivor identity. This can limit recovery and can sometimes create resistance to working on adult-centered recovery tasks.

4. Difficulty in sleeping or eating. Many children are abused in their own beds in the middle of the night, so that for adult survivors, nighttime becomes a trigger. Sleep is avoided because of the impending nightmares. Survivors may be chronically awakened as their body triggers memories of the nighttime abuse. They may rarely experience a deep, relaxing sleep as their bodies remain alert to danger. Such chronic sleep deprivation may need medical evaluation because if left un-interrupted, the survivor is prone to serious illness. Eating too little or too much is another aspect of this internal dysfunction. Abused children will sometimes starve themselves, believing their only control in life is over their food intake. Others tend to binge on food, hoping the extra weight will surround them with insulation designed to ward off the sexual interests of the offender. For others, food becomes a trigger, as in cult abuse where children are forced to ingest sacrificial substances.

5. Difficulty in coping with stress. As counselors we must be alert to the brain damage created by long-term alcohol or other drug poisoning. Not all the stress survivors undergo is due to their childhood histories. The physical recovery from chemicals generally takes one month for every year of active addiction. In addition to the stress of brain dysfunction, sur-vivors tend to deny their levels of stress and make few allowances for the additional stress created by the recovery process. One survivor told me her best coping mechanism for stress was "distraction therapy." The more stressed she be-came the more she did to avoid what stressed her. Levels of stress tend to build to such levels where common interventions (relaxation exercises, meditation) are nearly useless. Normal functioning becomes severely challenged.

6. Difficulty in placement of responsibility. During this phase of internal dysfunction, survivors become unable to believe they were abused and to place the responsibility on the offender. This denial is all-pervasive so that survivors tend to neglect basic needs and may even become self-destructive. They tell others they are fine and avoid the introspection necessary to realize their abuse as the root cause of their symptoms.

Over the next week John begins showing many of the signs of internal dysfunction. He finds that he can think of little else but his sexual experience with his brother. He has stopped thinking of it as abuse. He has trouble concentrating on his work for more than a few minutes at a time. Once he almost ran into a car as his mind was far from paying attention to the road. John is feeling so many emotions all at once: anger, fear, sadness, panic, and shame. Yet he cannot afford to let anyone know he's having a hard time dealing with them. He is irritable and increasingly depressed.

As time goes on, John remembers more and more of what his brother did to him. He remembers the abuse lasting for several years beginning when John was about nine and continuing until his brother went away to the military service—making John an adolescent when it stopped. John's shame increases. He has bad dreams of his brother laughing at him, so he stays up late avoiding going to sleep. He clings to his identity as a man and struggles out of bed each morning to get to work, accomplishing less and less each day. He has little appetite. He dwells on his memories and begins to believe that he must have done something to make his brother "come on" to him. In fact, he becomes sure that he was born a homosexual and at age nine was already seeking sexual contact.

External Dysfunction

If the internal problems are not acknowledged and managed in positive ways, survivors are likely to begin showing signs of their lives breaking down externally. This is a progression of behaviors and feeling states which occur after survivors have exhausted all their abilities in coping with the internal dysfunction. External dysfunction, like internal problems, can be caused from chronic buildup of stress and denial of the warning signs when they first began to occur. If survivors fail to deal with internal problems, it is just a matter of time before their lives begin to show serious difficulties. Let's examine the signs of external dysfunction:

1. Avoidance and symptomatic behaviors. Some survivors believe they feel bad because they sought out help and are now telling. They believe that it is because of the therapy that they now feel so bad. One way to feel better, they believe, is to avoid thinking about, feeling about, or talking about the abuse. When asked, they tend to be defensive and divert energy away from their abusive experiences. It is not uncommon for survivors to become more involved in someone else's recovery or difficulties at this point as another way of distraction. This is sometimes referred to as "working someone else's program." Counselors may notice that their client is using more time in their sessions talking about irrelevant issues rather than to feel pain. Some survivors, not content to simply avoid the issue, will indulge in risk-taking behavior, like driving too fast on the freeway or darting in and out of traffic. Compulsive behaviors such as overeating or unsafe sexual activity may be part of this stage. Impulsive behavior is also common, whether it is taking on way too much work or activity or whether it is engaging in high-risk behavior. Regardless, survivors will approach these activities with little concern for their own energy or safety. They tend to isolate themselves from others as well as fail to listen to their own inner voices about the consequences of their destructive behaviors.

2. Crisis-building. Considering the self-destructive behaviors the survivor is now engaged in, it is understandable that a crisis is just around the corner. Increasingly the survivor lives in an overfocused way, creating for herself inflexible work or school schedules, or losing daily schedules entirely. Old coping patterns emerge so that the survivor becomes vulnerable to re-victimizing situations. Unfortunately, many survivors find that being in a crisis is actually comforting, as the rush of adrenaline is so very familiar. Counselors are encouraged to gently confront the survivor who appears to be in constant crisis as merely a resistance to further resolving abuse issues.

3. Immobilization/depression. Survivors at this point feel stuck. They believe recovery is impossible. They believe they will always be victims. They may have numerous recovery tools but become unable to take any further action. They have decreasing amounts of energy necessary for their recovery which can become a true clinical depression. There may be changes exhibited in eating, sleeping, and certainly in the lack of joy. Magical thinking is common—wanting the benefits of recovery without being able or willing to put in the hard work and time necessary. I have referred to this as "beam-me-over therapy."

4. Hypervigilance and anxiety. As children, survivors had to watch the people around them for signs of impending danger. This vigilance shows up again now in an acute way so that anyone is seen as a potential threat. Survivors use all their available energy in protecting themselves, and attempting to persuade them that such amounts are unwarranted fall on deaf ears. As everyone becomes suspect, the survivor becomes easily irritated with friends and family members. There is an overreaction to feelings and upset comes all too easily. Chronic feelings of anxiety are common.

5. Social withdrawal. The survivor now actively avoids friends and family. Therapy sessions or group meetings may be avoided or dropped altogether. Twelve Step meetings may be dropped or considered unsupportive. The last place to suffer seems to be the workplace, although some survivors are so depressed, immobilized, and hypervigilant that they cannot continue to work effectively.

6. Confusion and overreaction. When survivors are using so much energy in surviving, it is no wonder their thinking becomes unclear. Survivors complain of too much input. They become confused and cannot focus on the simplest tasks. When they attempt to respond to something, it is often in a flood of overreaction. They tend to make mountains out of molehills or overfocus on irrelevant problems.

7. Learned helplessness. In a movie made for HBO called "Death Watch," prisoners are paired with another anonymous prisoner. Each wears a neck band which will explode if either partner goes farther than 100 yards from the other. This type of victimization is commonly felt in survivors who feel they cannot tread past certain limits within their perception. Learned helplessness comes from their inability to change in any way their abusive experience coupled with their position of insubordination. They are unable to seek help and avoid or "bite" the hand that does reach out to them. Seeking comfort in familiarity, survivors at this stage may seek out or remain in offending situations or continue to be around offending people.

John has a break from his memories and he has a much needed breather. During this time he feels a little better and decides his problem is that he's neglected his family. To compensate he spends the weekend taking his children to the zoo, his wife out to dinner, and frantically doing yard work. At the end of the weekend he notices that he's actually not feeling better at all, that he is just trying harder not to think about it. On Sunday evening he goes for a drive alone. He gets that "spacey" feeling, and when he "comes to" he's going 90 mph and closing in on a semitrailer-truck. Terrified, he returns home at 2:00 a.m. His wife tries to talk to him, asking about his changing behavior. John dares not tell her what's going on for fear she will be revolted by what he has done with his brother. He tells her he is just under a little pressure but that otherwise he is fine.

On Monday morning John can hardly get out of bed. He is very depressed and anxious. He has fantasies that his male co-workers are going to come on to him. He thinks about all the potential offenders in his AA group and changes his meeting place. Twice he got lost trying to find the meeting and he's wondering if he has the energy to continue going. Things at home are increasingly tense. John found himself yelling at his son for leaving a toy lying around, then yelling at his wife for "babying" the boy. He just walks away when his wife tries to talk to him about what's going on.

Loss of Control

If the symptoms of external dysfunction are left uninterrupted, behavioral loss of control will begin to occur. During this period survivors become unable to control their behavior or care for themselves adequately. They continue to strengthen their denial, and problems increase to crisis proportions.

1. Loss of boundaries. Abused children are taught there are no boundaries. In adulthood the violation of boundaries and victimization of the survivor sometimes continues from family members. This might take the form of inappropriate or offensive contacts by the perpetrator or demands made by the family for perpetrator loyalty. Survivors may act out by letting down their own boundaries and making inappropriate demands on their children, such as asking them to take on more household duties, care for younger children, or become the survivor's emotional confidante. Boundaries are also lost when the survivor gives credit or power to another's opinion of them as being "crazy" as an explanation of this difficult time.

2. Poor judgment. Abused children deal with the confusion of being abused by reversing the truth: Their perpetrator is good and they are bad. Therefore, as children they are given no way of learning good judgment. They deny that they are in danger from current perpetrators and deny that they might be in danger from their own self-destructive behaviors, their self-neglect, or through their environment. They make poor choices in regard to people and places and are vulnerable to re-victimization.

3. Inability to seek help. At this point the survivor is isolating herself. Offers of help are refused or there is denial of the need for help. She refuses to offer herself any further options for care and comfort.

4. Acting on destructive impulses. The shame and self-blame have once again kicked in and self-destructive behaviors are inevitable. This takes the form of self-mutilation (cutting, burning, or in other ways harming oneself), high risk-taking, and life-threatening activities such as going on a sexual binge. Feelings of self-loathing are high.

5. Option reduction. Survivors feel now that they are trapped by their pain and their inability to manage their lives. They feel there is no way out other than insanity, suicide, or chemical use. They feel overwhelmed with helplessness and hopelessness and have an intense fear of losing everything in their lives or of dying.

6. Emotional or physical collapse. With the loss of options coupled with the refusal for help, survivors will have an emotional or physical breakdown. This takes the form of major panic attacks, psychosis, or severe depression, or the development of a serious disease or disorder such as chronic fatigue syndrome, heart disease, or lupus. Chronic conditions such as migraines or gastrointestinal disorders are often aggravated.

7. Re-victimization and reenactment. As the survivor has such poor judgment coupled with loss of boundaries and emotional collapse, re-victimizations are common (rape, assaults, neglect) as are reenacting experiences, where common situations feel emotionally similar to the original trauma. Defensive behaviors are set into motion.

Weeks go by as John continues to plunge into depression. He is increasingly confused, lacks concentration, and acts impulsively. He rarely talks to his family and isolates himself in his study after dinner. Once his son came into the study and John took him on his lap. John proceeded to burst into tears. When his wife found them John was saying something about how he would kill anyone who tried to touch their son. She quickly took the boy to the other room. John was unable to talk coherently with her. She offered to take him to see his counselor the next day. He refused, saying he had vowed he could do this without anyone's help. She suggested going with him to meetings, visiting with his beloved sister, or taking a few days off work. John refused to do anything differently. Overwhelmed, John felt helpless and trapped by his confusion and pain. He believed he was going crazy.

A week later John left work early and drove to a bar on the other side of town. He had a soda and sat there trying to think of how to get himself to feel better. While he was sitting there a man sat down next to him. He was a man younger than John, very good looking. He struck up a conversation with John, and the two talked for an hour. John felt like he was understood. When the man invited John to his apartment for dinner John didn't hesitate.

After a wonderful meal John noticed it was 10:30 and realized he hadn't called his wife. He thanked the man for the evening and attempted to leave. The man stopped him at the door and made it very clear that he wanted John to have sex with him. John panicked. The two struggled and John eventually broke free. But in the process the man had fondled his genitals. John returned home, crawled into bed fully clothed, and lay there staring at the ceiling.

Deterioration
The end result of this terrifying series of losses of control is deterioration.

1. Suicide/homicide attempts. Survivors may make serious attempts to kill themselves through overdoses, cutting major blood vessels, or by shooting themselves. Occasionally survivors will make a homicide threat, although it is usually rare—they are much more likely to take out their rage on themselves.

2. Debilitating shame. The survivor's self-blame and self-loathing become so great that immobilization occurs. Acting on this shame is common through self-destructive behaviors.

3. Abuse reenactment. The survivor is frequently re-victimized in numerous ways.

4. Life-threatening problems. The survivor's life is so impaired that he is threatened physically, emotionally, socially, and occupationally.

5. Relapse to chemical addiction. If the survivor has not already returned to chemical use, she does so now strongly with an "I don't care" attitude. Intervention is next to impossible at this time.

6. Retreat into pathology. This is the point at which the survivor has a true psychiatric or medical crisis.

John believes he has few options other than suicide, insanity, or a return to drinking. The morning after the assault, John leaves for work but instead goes to a discount store and buys a gun. He places it on the passenger seat and drives to the nearest bar. He orders double scotches and sits thinking. After six drinks he believes he has the courage to commit suicide. But upon leaving the bar he runs into the side of a car in the parking lot and can't move his car any farther. The owner rushes out and police are called. John, who is obviously intoxicated, cannot explain the presence of the gun. He is driven by police to a local hospital where his wife is called. John is evaluated carefully and admitted to the psychiatric unit for evaluation.

Chapter 5

Relapse Prevention Planning

Many of you may have turned to this section of the book long before finishing the relapse progression simply because you were getting quite depressed seeing how the process can go! Fortunately, relapse can be interrupted if both the survivor and counselor know what to look for and how to intervene in what can be a lethal process. Chemically dependent survivors have a strong tendency toward chemical and self-destructive relapse. Many relapse because they don't understand the process of recovery and its stuck places, and they don't know what to do to prevent relapse. Appropriate action by the survivor and his or her support system can interrupt if not prevent relapse before the consequences become tragic. Planning for relapse can create for the survivor a "safety net." She knows what her early warning signs are and can develop a plan of action for interrupting the relapse process once it begins. The following steps are included in relapse prevention planning:

1. Stablization—Regaining Control

Once the survivor has begun to slip into a relapse progression it becomes important to stop and "get a grip." The tasks are very similar to the stabilization tasks of recovery covered early in this book. It is helpful for the survivor to re-prioritize his life to include only the essential. Much of his energy now needs to go into containment, self-control, and reaching out for help. Because obsessive thinking may be a part of the survivor's problems now, containers can be offered such as creating safe places for emotional discharge, safe people with whom to discuss the relapse process, and visualizations of internal retreats. It is helpful to remind survivors that *the abuse is not happening now,* that they are adults and can make active choices for their safety and nurturance.

Other peers in recovery can be essential in helping the survivor place her experience in perspective by sharing their own relapse process and steps they took toward regaining control. If a recovery contract has been created in previous counseling sessions, it may be time to activate it. (A recovery contract outlines instructions for others if the survivor begins to relapse, such as driving the survivor to an inpatient treatment center.)This may mean asking for more help, increasing counseling sessions or group meetings, or getting more rest. It also may be helpful for the survivor to hear that "this too shall pass," preferably from another recovering survivor.

2. Assessment—Figuring Out What Happened

It is important that the survivor, once stablized so that he has more control over his thinking and emotions, try to understand what happened that caused the relapse process to begin in the first place. It might be useful to go through the Sexual Trauma Checklist to determine if there is a particular task the survivor is up against and feeling stuck. Does he understand the task? Does he have enough support in mastering the task? Has he skipped over earlier recovery tasks which leave him unsupported now to continue developmentally in recovery?

Because triggers abound for most survivors, it is common that a relapse process can begin by an unmanaged trigger. An example might be a situation in which the survivor receives an upsetting phone call from an offending family member and neglects to tell anyone or process the feelings that were created. It is also important to ask how well the survivor has been taking care of herself. This particularly applies to advising the survivor not to get too hungry, angry, lonely, or tired.

Many survivors I work with will begin a relapse process simply by getting into a cycle of self-neglect. Such simple monitoring of asking how well they are sleeping, eating, and managing the demands of work or parenting can be very useful. It is helpful to refer survivors to their high-risk factors, acknowledge how these present particular difficulty, and make accomodations for them. Explain that we wouldn't ask someone who has recently had surgery to return to work and have optimal performance. Lastly, it is always useful to try to assess if this particular relapse process is unique in its progression or a replay of other relapses. Chances are, there will be similarities to this and other relapses so that there may be a wealth of information to be learned.

3. Education

Working with sexual trauma survivors requires some degree of teaching therapy. It is essential that survivors learn about the process of recovery and how relapse occurs— whether chemical relapse, self-destructive, or PTSD relapse. They need to understand what post traumatic stress disorder and post acute withdrawal are and how they irritate recovery. It may be helpful to recommend some reading materials for survivors. There are many books and articles that provide specific tools for recovery or accounts of other survivors. The involvement of others is critical. Denial and minimization of the abuse and its aftereffects can be a trigger to begin relapse, and contact and challenge by other survivors can interrupt these defenses. Survivors need to be encouraged to focus on their *similarities* to others, not their differences.

4. Warning Sign Identification

Warning signs are those "red flags" that recovering people need to be aware of on a daily basis which, if poorly managed, can begin the relapse process. These may be problems outside or inside the self. They are often triggered by specific high-risk situations. A complete curriculum of warning sign identification is listed in Terry Gorski's *Staying Sober Workbook*, which I encourage both counselors and survivors to read and work through. For those who are unable to complete such a comprehensive process, the following steps are recommended:

- Review with the survivor the 37 warning signs listed by Terry Gorski, or review the 40 warning signs listed in this book. They appear at the bottom of the grid as the relapse progression.
- Have the survivor star no more than five warning signs that apply to him or her.
- Ask the survivor then to rewrite the five (or fewer) warning signs in his or her own words.
- Now ask the survivor to tell you a story about a situation in which that particular warning sign manifested and then a story about a future event that is likely to create for the survivor the same warning sign.
- Next ask the survivor to identify the thoughts, feelings, and compelling actions that occur with the warning sign.

After this process, the survivor is ready to move to the next part of relapse planning, that of learning to manage the warning signs.

5. Warning Sign Management

Once warning signs are identified, an action plan must be created for constructive thinking, emotional management, and behavioral change. First, it is important for the survivor to identify, predict, plan for, and master trigger events either by attempting to avoid them or integrating them into daily life. High-risk factors must also be identified and accommodated. Generally it is easier for people to do something different rather than to change the way they think or feel about it. A daily schedule is helpful which includes activities that support recovery and allows for triggers and high-risk situations. Of course, this means showing up for recovery rather than slipping into the denial that is so common. Even small changes in behavior can go a long way toward changing thoughts and feelings.

6. Daily Review of Recovery

Survivors tend to be so depressed that there is little daily structure to their lives, or so full of activity that there is no time for self-care. Relapse prevention means planning on a daily basis activities which will help to manage difficult situations, memories, or feelings. Activities might include attending counseling or a support group, writing in a journal, writing letters to oneself or to offenders, or creating and using affirmations of self-worth and self-forgiveness. Survivors tend to get an idea and beat it to death, so that they have a hard time acknowledging when something is simply not working. I have often asked, "Are you tired of running yourself into a brick wall?" Survivors need constant reassurance that they have numerous options.

7. Involve Significant Others

There are excellent worksheets in both the *Staying Sober Workbook* and *Courage to Heal Workbook* that ask about the safety and availability of significant others. Through a writing process survivors can identify for themselves people who could be supportive in their recovery process. These people, once identified, need to be informed of the survivor's particular warning signs with specific instructions on intervention. For example, one survivor explained to a good friend how she often dissociated. She described how she looked and acted when this happened and asked her friend to call her name or touch her shoulder if she saw the survivor acting in this way. Such a system of support can and should expand beyond a few close friends, partners, or family members. Such a relapse prevention network could include Twelve Step groups, counselors, doctors such as family physicians or psychologists, inpatient units and treatment centers for psychiatric emergencies or intensive emotional work, and therapy groups. Community hot lines and counseling phone lines are also helpful, as are workshops and seminars on a variety of recovery issues. Most important is the survivor's willingness to be open and honest with those in the relapse network and to change the makeup of the group if supportive feedback is not forthcoming.

8. Follow-up and Reinforcement

Life is ever-changing. Just when you think you've about figured out a problem in your life and things are going smoothly, life gives you another challenge. Consequently, new warning signs may emerge over time, so that the relapse prevention planning must undergo revision every few months.

Chapter 6
Getting Help

Recovery *is* possible. It starts when survivors admit and accept that they were abused as children and that they are affected in many areas of their lives today. Recovery is supported by learning about the process, understanding how PTSD and chemical addiction are interrelated and can irritate one another, and recognizing how relapse can be prevented. Recovering from chemical addiction or from childhood trauma is difficult. Recovering from *both* issues simultaneously may seem impossible. However, such dual recovery may be essential. Getting the right help can make the difference between successful, thorough recovery or a low-level sobriety with chronic relapses. What follows are ways survivors have found to get the critical help they need.

1. Abstinence

It is impossible to go about seeking help if the survivor is addicted. I have said to many survivors, "Memories are terribly painful, but feelings won't kill you as your addiction will." As long as the survivor continues to use chemicals, she will be unable to sort out how many of her problems are related to her use and what is related to her abuse issues. Abstinence helps in focusing on what problems are connected to what disorder.

2. Identifying Oneself as a Chemically Dependent Abuse Survivor

Denial is prominent in both addiciton and in abuse. It is important that survivors admit and eventually accept their disease and trauma history and honor their special needs. Old coping defenses can be reframed as understandable ways of dealing with overwhelming obstacles. New options open up for survivors who allow themselves to appreciate how their strengths have come from surviving such experiences.

3. Learning to Take Care

Laura Davis, author of *Courage to Heal,* says that survivors often ask her how to know if they are moving along in recovery. Her answer is not to ask how many memories they have had or whether they have confronted the perpetrator, but to ask how well they are taking care of themselves. Abuse as a child becomes part of the way the survivors continue to treat themselves. Learning to soothe, comfort, and take care of oneself is crucial in recovery. Because abused children are often neglected, self-care may mean starting out with the basics—by learning to eat well, to exercise, to develop a routine sleep pattern, to manage stress, and so on. No matter whether the survivor is working on warning signs connected to her addiction or her abuse, being able to take care of herself is the foundation of recovery.

4. Getting Help from Others

Attending Twelve Step groups such as AA and NA will serve as a foundation support for staying sober. A survivor's attention to his addiction is the most important focus early in recovery. Listening to others share their courage, strength, and hope goes a long way toward facing and accepting the disease of chemical addiction. Attending meetings can also help in learning how to speak openly and honestly about one's experience. Developing trust in such groups can take time, so survivors are encouraged to "keep coming back" and to take small, manageable risks. In addition to attending meetings, obtaining a sponsor can be helpful. Choosing a sponsor who is also a survivor can be helpful as long as this person is further along in recovery than the survivor.

It is important that the survivor feel safe and understood by a sponsor and that the sponsor know the dynamics of PTSD and addiction. Some survivors find it is easier to work with a sponsor of their same gender, or who is not the same gender of the person who abused them. Another very important way of getting help is through professional counseling. The search for a counselor can be a time-consuming process, but considering that the survivor may be working with this person for several years, it is a process well worth considering. A qualified therapist can help survivors move through painful memory work, provide essential support, and teach critical self-care skills. For the chemically addicted survivor I believe it is important that the therapist be skilled in both the treatment of addictions as well as the treatment of childhood trauma. Because relapse for survivors is such a strong possibility, I would also suggest that the therapist have training in—or preferably be certified in— relapse prevention therapy. The questions listed below serve as a guide in seeking a qualified therapist:

1. What are your professional counseling qualifications? (If the survivor doesn't understand the answer she needs to ask.)

2. How long have you been a counselor?

3. What kind of problems and issues do you treat?

4. What is your treatment approach?

5. What is your feeling about medication?

6. Do you understand and support Twelve Step work?

7. What is your experience with relapse?

8. What brought you to this type of counseling?

9. How long would my treatment last?

10. Are you yourself in recovery? (optional)

11. Are you yourself a survivor? (optional)

Another resource for getting help is group therapy. Many groups exist, from structured relapse prevention therapy groups, to incest therapy groups, to codependency and family-of-origin therapy groups. It is important that the survivor choose which group is most likely to support those issues that are most troublesome at a given time. For instance, one survivor might begin treatment in an intensive outpatient program for early chemical addiction recovery. Then she might go into a long-term, open-ended sexual trauma therapy group. Along with this, the survivor would be attending Twelve Step groups and perhaps a relapse prevention support group. At times when the survivor might be feeling overwhelmed or suicidal, brief hospitalization could be warranted. Choosing a hospital that has a sexual trauma component can be very helpful. Some hospitals offer free aftercare groups for survivors. It is important that the survivor carefully monitor her needs and seek groups out accordingly.

Conclusion

Recovery *is* possible. By understanding the developmental process, trusting that process, and recognizing the potential for relapse, survivors are very likely to move into productive, meaningful, and happy lives. It is important and essential work for counselors. I can think of a no more meaningful time than when I received a wedding invitation from a once frightened, distrustful woman who never believed anyone could love her. Or the birth announcement from a man who thought he could never parent. The value of this work comes not from loud, public expressions of victory but from the very private experience of the small changes that lead a survivor to care for herself or find reason to live. It is long, draining work, but well worth it. It helps to have Faith.

Faith

When you have come to the edge
of all the light you know
And are about to step off into the
darkness of the unknown
Faith is knowing one of two things will happen
There will be something solid to stand on
Or you will be taught how to fly.

Anonymous

References

1. Stefani Atwood, personal communication (1988).

2. Ellen Bass and Laura Davis, *The Courage to Heal: A Guide for Women Survivors of Child Sexual Abuse* (Harper & Row, 1988).

3. E. Sue Blume, *Secret Survivors: Uncovering Incest & Its Aftereffects* (John Wiley & Sons, 1990).

4. John Briere, *Therapy for Adults Molested as Children: Beyond Survival* (Springer, 1989).

5. Christine Courtois, *Healing the Incest Wound: Adult Survivors in Therapy* (Norton, 1988).

6. P. Crigler, "Incest in the Military Family," in Florence W. Kaslow and Richard I. Ridenour, eds, *The Military Family: Dynamics & Treatment* (Guilford, 1984).

7. J. A. Kovach, "The relationship between treatment failures of alcoholic women and incestuous histories with possible implications for post-traumatic stress disorder symptomatology," *Dissertation Abstracts International* 44 (3-A): 710.

8. Wayne Kritsberg, *The Adult Children of Alcoholics Syndrome* (Bantam Books, 1985).

9. Ellen Ratner, *The Other Side of the Family: A Workbook about Abuse, Incest, & Neglect* (Health Communications, 1990).

10. D. J. Rohsenow, R. Corbett, and D. Devine, "Molested as Children: A Hidden Contribution to Substance Abuse?" *Journal of Substance Abuse Treatment* 5 (1988): 13-18.

11. Diana Russell, *The Secret Trauma: Incest in the Lives of Girls and Women* (Basic Books, 1986).

Bibliography

Bass, Ellen, and Laura Davis. *The Courage to Heal: A Guide for Women Survivors of Child Sexual Abuse.* Harper & Row, 1988.

Briere, John. *Therapy for Adults Molested as Children: Beyond Survival.* Springer, 1989.

Burgess, Ann, et al. *Sexual Assault of Children and Adolescents.* D.C. Health, 1978.

Courtois, Christine. *Healing the Incest Wound: Adult Survivors in Therapy.* Norton, 1988.

Davis, Laura. *The Courage to Heal Workbook.* Harper & Row, 1990.

Everstine, Diana, and Louis Everstine. *Sexual Trauma in Children and Adolescents: Dynamics and Treatment.* Brunner-Mazel, 1989.

Figley, Charles R., ed. *Trauma and Its Wake, Volume 1: The Study and Treatment of Post-Traumatic Stress Disorder.* Brunner Mazel, 1985; *Volume 2: Traumatic Stress Theory, Research, and Intervention.* Brunner-Mazel, 1986.

Gannon, J. Patrick. *Soul Survivors: A New Beginning for Adults Abused as Children.* Prentice-Hall, 1989.

Gil, Eliana. *Treatment of Adult Survivors of Childhood Abuse.* Launch Press, 1988.

Goodwin, Jean M. *Sexual Abuse: Incest Victims and Their Families.* Yearbook Medical, 1989.

Gorski, Terence T., and Merlene Miller. *Staying Sober: A Guide for Relapse Prevention.* Herald House/Independence Press, 1986.

Gorski, Terence T. *The Staying Sober Workbook: A Serious Solution for the Problem of Relapse.* Herald House/Independence Press, 1988.

Gorski, Terence T. *Passages through Recovery: An Action Plan for Preventing Relapse.* Hazelden, 1989.

Herman, Judith Lewis. *Father-Daughter Incest.* Harvard Press, 1981.

Laws, Richard. *Relapse Prevention with Sex Offenders.* Guilford, 1989.

Lew, Mike. *Victims No Longer: Men Recovering from Incest and Other Childhood Sexual Abuse.* Harper & Row, 1990.

Maltz, Wendy, and Beverly Holman, *Incest and Sexuality: A Guide to Understanding and Healing.* Lexington, 1987.

Russell, Diana. *The Secret Trauma: Incest in the Lives of Girls and Women.* Basic Books, 1986.

Sgroi, Suzanne. *Handbook of Clinical Intervention in Child Sexual Abuse.* Lexington, 1981.

Smith, Michelle. *Michelle Remembers.* Pocket Books, 1980.

Utain, Marsha, and Barbara Oliver. *Scream Louder: Through Hell and Healing with an Incest Survivor and Her Therapist.* Health Communications, 1989.

Weissberg, Michael. *Dangerous Secrets: Maladaptive Responses to Stress.* Norton, 1983.

Appendix

A. The Surviving to Thriving Continuum

A Developmental Model of Recovery for Survivors of Sexual Abuse

Based Upon the CENAPS Model of Treatment and developed by Caryl Trotter, M.A. and Stefani Atwood, M.A. with Terence T. Gorski

B. The Developmental Model of Recovery from Sexual Trauma Checklist

C. Relapse Warning Signs for Chemically Dependent Sexual Abuse Survivors

The Recovery Process

Trapped	Hope	Reassessment	Integration	Validation	Emergence
Simply Surviving	**Stabilization**	**Early Recovery**	**Middle Recovery**	**Late Recovery**	**Growth/Development**
1. Increased symptoms	1. Recognizing self-destructiveness	1. Developing trust & self-awareness	1. Recognizing abusive family system	1. Confronting / separating	1. Daily confrontation of brainwashing
2. Family crisis	2. Managing shock & stress	2. Creating realistic "safety nets"	2. Reassigning responsibility	2. Expressing feelings appropriately	2. Identifying Trigger Symptom Cycle
3. Memory triggers	3. Acknowledging sexual abuse	3. Understanding abuse as root of symptoms	3. Grieving multiple losses	3. Developing a self	3. Healthy emotional expression
4. Developmental blocks	4. Recognizing chronic survival patterns	4. Catharisis of repressed memories / feelings	4. Examine support systems	4. Becoming a choice-maker	4. Creating a self-enhancing life-style
5. Failing coping mechanisms	5. Developing hope & motivation	5. Honor childhood survival strategies	5. Challenge learned helplessness	5. Establishing intimate relationships	5. Effectively managing life's transitions
					6. Expanding intimacy

Surviving → → → → → **Thriving**

Surviving → → → → → → **Thriving**

Trouble Spots in Recovery

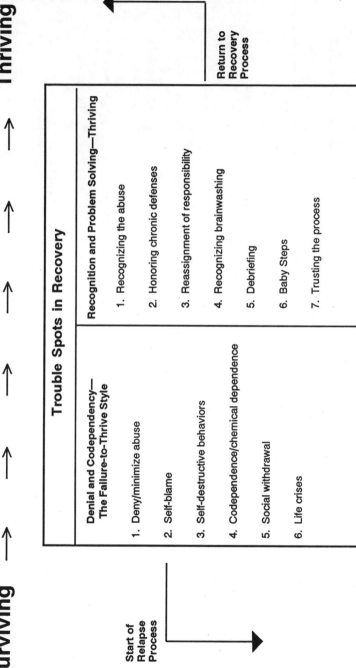

**Denial and Codependency—
The Failure-to-Thrive Style**

1. Deny/minimize abuse

2. Self-blame

3. Self-destructive behaviors

4. Codependence/chemical dependence

5. Social withdrawal

6. Life crises

Recognition and Problem Solving—Thriving

1. Recognizing the abuse

2. Honoring chronic defenses

3. Reassignment of responsibility

4. Recognizing brainwashing

5. Debriefing

6. Baby Steps

7. Trusting the process

Return to Recovery Process

Start of Relapse Process

The Relapse Process

High Risk Factors	Trigger Events	Internal Dysfunction	External Dysfunction	Loss of Control	Deterioration
		Difficulty in . . .			
1. Severe PTSD	1. PTSD	1. Thinking clearly	1. Avoidance and symptomatic behaviors	1. Loss of boundaries	1. Suicide/homicide attempts
2. Torture / cults	2. Reactions to disclosures	2. Managing emotions	2. Crisis building	2. Poor judgment	2. Debilitating shame
3. Victim life-style	3. Re-victimization	3. Managing memories	3. Immobilization / depression	3. Inability to seek help	3. Abuse reenactment
4. Social isolation	4. Sexual encounters	4. Sleep and/or eating	4. Hypervigilance and anxiety	4. Acting on destructive impulses	4. Life-threatening problems
5. Self-neglect	5. Abandonment	5. Coping with stress	5. Social withdrawal	5. Option reduction	5. Substance abuse
6. Recanting	6. Changes and choices	6. Placement of responsibility	6. Confusion and overreaction	6. Emotional and/or physical collapse	6. Retreat into pathology
7. Flight into health/resistance	7. Other familial disclosures		7. Learned helplessness	7. Re-victimization and reenactment	

Appendix B

The Developmental Model of Recovery from Sexual Trauma Checklist

The following checklist was developed for counselors as an assessment tool to be used with clients who have been sexually traumatized. The checklist should be used in an interview setting. Explain to the client that recovery is developmental, that recovering from sexual trauma is a process of growth and development that progresses from basic to more complex tasks over time. Attempting the more complex tasks while bypassing or avoiding the more basic tasks sets the stage for stuck points along the way to recovery. Sometimes the stuck points for trauma survivors can become serious, life-threatening problems.

As counselors you are encouraged to provide this checklist early in the recovery process. You will have already completed an initial assessment of the presenting problem and recognized that the client's sexual abuse issues warrant direct treatment.

Go through the checklist item by item asking of the client in your own words if he or she has accomplished the stated task. For example, by asking about the tasks during the transition stage you will discover just how depleted and symptomatic the client has become. During stabilization you will get a sense of whether the client has already begun to ask for help, has learned any self-soothing techniques to manage stress, and has come to some basic understanding of the dynamics of post traumatic stress disorder (a common diagnosis for survivors of trauma).

As you proceed through the checklist you will begin to notice that the client has not completed more and more tasks. It is at this point that you will begin to get a sense of what treatment issues will need to be addressed. Hence, the checklist becomes a basis for treatment planning. Failing to master certain developmental tasks does not necessarily mean the client will fail to recover. It does mean, however, that the client is less supported in her/his full recovery and may be prone to developing stuck points which can begin the relapse process.

The Developmental Model of Recovery from Sexual Trauma Checklist

Copyright © 1992
Caryl Trotter

I. Transition

1. Increased symptoms
   __ a. Progressively more severe problems
   __ b. Self-destructive or self-defeating behaviors
   __ c. Attempts at problem-solving

2. Family crisis
   __ a. Abuse reenactments
   __ b. Threats of abandonment by important persons
   __ c. Marital or relationship problems

3. Memory triggers
   __ a. Flashbacks, nightmares, intrusive images
   __ b. Memories interfere with functioning
   __ c. Disturbing, upsetting memories

4. Developmental blocks
   __ a. Unable to cope as mature adult
   __ b. Recognition of underdeveloped aspects of self
   __ c. Self-defeating life-style

5. Failing coping mechanisms
   __ a. Severely depressed, overwhelmed
   __ b. Denying and minimizing abuse issues
   __ c. Repressed memories surfacing

II. Stabilization

1. Recognizes self-destructiveness
   __ a. Recognizes need for outside help
   __ b. Recognizes self-directed aggression
   __ c. Recognizes inner talk that is self-defeating, self-destructive

2. Manages shock and stress
   __ a. Recovers from shock of realizing trauma of abuse
   __ b. Reduces stress to a minimum
   __ c. Receives PTSD education and management techniques

3. Acknowledges sexual abuse
   __ a. Accomplishes stages of acknowledgment: denying > considering > bargaining acknowledgment > resolution
   __ b. Verbalizes sexual abuse memories as presented (bits and pieces, whole scenes, sensory memories, hunches, etc.)

4. Creates realistic safety nets
   __ a. Seeks safe people and places to disclose abuse memories and experiences
   __ b. Creates safe containers for trauma memory work
   __ c. Creates recovery contract

5. Develops hope and motivation
   __ a. Identifies with survivor peers
   __ b. Identifies abuse issues as a core reason for life problems

___ c. Releases emotion through abuse
       disclosures

III. Early Recovery

1. Develops trust and self-awareness
___ a. Receives external validation (belief) of
       abuse memories and perceptions
___ b. Focuses on inner process
___ c. Learns to trust in self-perceptions of trauma
       as validated through abuse aftereffects and
       symptoms
___ d. Becomes self-directed vs. other-directed

2. Recognizes chronic survival patterns
___ a. Honors defenses created as an abused child
       to cope with trauma
___ b. Assesses current coping mechanisms as to
       adaptive or maladaptive
___ c. Challenges ways of thinking, feeling, and
       acting as to current usefulness

3. Acknowledges abuse as source of symptoms
___ a. Understands family system as deterrent
       to normal growth
___ b. Views symptoms as normal reactions to
       abnormal situations

4. Catharsis of repressed memories and feelings
___ a. Breaks the secret of abuse to a safe person
___ b. Releases feelings attached to trauma
___ c. Understands complex process of how
       traumatic memory is stored and released

___ d. Becomes comfortable with own unique
     memory release process and accompanying
     feelings

5. Honors Childhood Strategies
___ a. Lists coping mechanisms connected to
     surviving abuse
___ b. Reframes current symptoms as survival
     mechanisms
___ c. Becomes aware of traumatized child-self
     frozen in time (chronic shock)

IV. Middle Recovery

1. Understanding of abusive family system
___ a. Completes a serious investigation into family
     system
___ b. Understands generationality of abuse
___ c. Acknowledges lack of protection and
     abandonment by caregivers

2. Reassigning responsibility
___ a. Places responsibility for abuse onto
     perpetrator(s)
___ b. Engages in active anger work
___ c. Separates emotionally/physically from
     abusive family system

3. Grieving multiple losses
    a. Accepts reality of all losses (innocence,
     sexuality, childhood)
___ b. Emotionally expresses grief
___ c. Reinvests energy

4. Examines support systems
__ a. Evaluates intimate relationships
__ b. Evaluates roles in family (of creation and of origin)
__ c. Evaluates work roles and relationships
__ d. Evaluates relationships with recovering friends and peers

5. Challenges learned helplessness
__ a. Awareness of no longer being a victim
__ b. Awareness of choices
__ c. Acting on those healthy choices

V. Late Recovery

1. Confrontation and separation from offending family
__ a. Declares outrage and challenges family's denial
__ b. Initiates actual or symbolic confrontation
__ c. Initiates actual or symbolic separation to activate new identity

2. Expresses feelings appropriately
__ a. Acknowledges all emotions
__ b. Labels emotions
__ c. Expresses feelings appropriately (with approiate persons, places, times)

3. Develops a self
__ a. Exerts the power of identity through a working awareness of personal choices

4. Becomes a choice-maker
___ a. Expresses self
___ b. Examines spirituality

VI. Growth and Development

1. Daily confrontation of brainwashing

2. Identifies trigger-symptom cycle
___ a. Identifies stimuli which trigger trauma-
   connected reactions
___ b. Communicates triggers to support people,
   asks for support
___ c. Avoids or integrates triggers

3. Healthy emotional expression
___ a. Locates safe people and safe places
___ b. Enjoys full range of emotional expression
___ c. Initiates self-enhancing life-style through
   balanced physical, emotional, and spiritual
   support
___ d. Effectively manages life transitions
___ e. Expands intimacy

Appendix C

Relapse Warning Signs for Chemically Dependent Sexual Abuse Survivors

The following is a list of warning signs that adult survivors of sexual abuse have indicated were particularly difficult for them. Not attending early to such warning signs can lead the survivor to relapse to chemical use, severe post traumatic stress symptoms, or self-destructive behavior.

Read over the list along with the brief descriptions of each warning sign. Mark up to five of the signs with which you identify. Rewrite each of the warning signs you have marked in your own words. What makes warning signs easy to identify is the ability to make the descriptions very personal and unique to your own experience.

Phase I: Internal Warning Signs of Relapse

During this phase survivors experience difficulty in functioning normally within themselves. Some common symptoms are:

1. Difficulty in thinking clearly. The survivor has difficulty concentrating on even simple tasks. He may spend hours obsessing over a memory, anticipating danger and how he will respond to it, or dwelling on situations which are minor to most other people. This difficulty may be caused by physical deprivation such as lack of food or sleep, or from PTSD symptoms that are evident in survivors of trauma.

2. Difficulty in managing emotions. The feelings associated with being abused stuffed far away inside now begin emerging. Survivors feel too much, or too little, or the wrong feeling for the situation. They may overreact to people and experiences or misjudge events. Oftentimes they feel their emotions are "childish," which is quite accurate since the feelings are those the child felt at the time of the trauma but which were never expressed. This roller coaster of emotion leads some to believe they're going crazy.

3. Difficulty in managing memories. When the memories of childhood trauma return they can trigger the same thoughts, feelings, and behaviors as a child. For an adult this can be frightening. Memories may return in bits and pieces with little or no emotion attached. They may return in dreams or nightmares, or in unconnected images. Sometimes the body hurts where it was sexually abused, with no image or emotion connected. Survivors may be flooded with memories and find them terribly disruptive to their lives.

4. Difficulty in managing sleeping and eating. The emerging memories tend to make sleeping difficult so that survivors sleep too little, too much, or avoid sleep due to impending nightmares. Eating disorders are triggered and survivors tend to use food to numb themselves. Survivors eat too much with the intention of insulating and comforting themselves, or eat too little to attempt to de-sexualize themselves to create the illusion of protection.

5. Difficulty in coping with stress. Survivors tend to deny that they are under stress and cope with it by neglecting it, acting self-destructively, adding on *more* stress, or by becoming so busy they don't have time to feel how stressful their lives have become. Many survivors are molested when they are in bed so that being relaxed becomes paired with being vulnerable. Times of peace and serenity for many survivors provoke anxiety.

6. Difficulty in the placement of responsibility. Abuse happens and is maintained by the skillfulness of the perpetrator telling the victim that he or she is to blame and that bad things will happen if he or she tells. Survivors incorporate this belief so that they continue to blame themselves as adults. They have great difficulty in solving the discrepancy between who the perpetrator was supposed to have been to them and how they really were to the child. Survivors believe that they are bad and accept responsibility for the abuse.

Phase II: External Warnings Signs of Relapse

During this phase survivors begin showing problems outside of themselves. These occur after they have exhausted all their abilities to cope with their internal difficulties. Some common symptoms are:

1. Avoidant and symptomatic behaviors. Survivors will attempt to distract themselves from thinking, feeling, or talking about their abuse experiences or memories. They may become defensive when asked how they are doing, or change the subject if asked about their abuse. They may use their counseling sessions to focus on irrelevent issues. They may begin to avoid people or situations that could be supportive. They may become compulsive, impulsive, or engage in high-risk behavior.

2. Crisis-building. During this phase survivors begin to experience a sequence of events caused by avoiding the effects of their abuse, by isolating, and by neglecting their recovery program. They tend to be overfocused on small problems, quickly blowing them out of proportion. Feelings of impending doom sometimes prevail, and some begin to experience symptoms of depression. They may begin to lose their daily structure and be unable to plan constructively. Plans become more ideas and wishful hopes than reality.

3. Immobilization/depression. This is a period where the survivor feels stuck. She is unable to initiate action and feels she is controlled by events in the world rather than having much control over those events. A sense of failure is felt about recovery in general, believing that it is too hard or impossible for her. She believes she will always be this way—a depressed, hopeless victim. Some survivors simply want to get better without going through the hard work necessary for recovery, preferring to be "beamed over" into health. Much energy is used in this time of wishful thinking and as feelings of depression increase.

4. Hypervigilance and anxiety. This is a sense that anyone is a potential danger to the survivor. Relationships become strained with friends, family, counselors, and supportive people. The survivor feels hurt and confused when others make comments about his changing behavior, and he discounts others who may try to reach out to him. Feelings of anxiety are strong as the survivor waits to be abused, victimized, or betrayed.

5. Social withdrawal. They begin to spend more and more time alone, believing no one can help them. Survivors can usually come up with many good reasons for avoiding people, but this only heightens the belief they hold that people are increasingly dangerous and that recovery is impossible.

6. Confusion and overreaction. During this phase survivors have trouble thinking clearly. Coupled with the often confusing nature of emerging memories, survivors sometimes feel they are going crazy. They become easily irritable and overreact to small events in their lives. They can become easily angered, frustrated, and resentful over small things. The stress of chronic anxiety coupled with anger can lead to explosions of rage or violence.

7. Learned helplessness. This term has often been associated with the battered wives syndrome, where the victim of violence believes she is utterly helpless to change her situation. This is a learned response to chronic victimization and is completely understandable. During this period the survivor feels helpless and hopeless about changing her life. She is unable to seek help from others, and turns down help if it is offered. She stands a good chance of being re-victimized at this time.

Phase III: Loss of Control

If the symptoms of external dysfunction are left uninterrupted, behavioral loss of control will begin to occur. During this period the survivor becomes unable to control her behavior or care for herself adequately. She continues to strengthen her denial and her problems increase to crisis proportions. Some of the common symptoms are:

1. Loss of boundaries. Survivors begin to question their rights for setting physical, sexual, emotional, and spiritual boundaries. They begin to believe that others have the right to ask them to do things that they would rather not do. Survivors feel guilty if they stand up for themselves and angry if they agree to something they know might jeopardize their recovery.

Some survivors find it hard to set any further sexual boundaries with their partners, particularly if they have had a previous agreement with them for temporary celibacy.

2. Poor judgment. They are unable to make good judgments about their own behavior and the behavior of others. They are drawn to people and places that are familiar to their dysfunctional family and often deny that they may be in danger from their environment or from their own self-neglect. Survivors make poor choices in who they spend their time with and where they go. Sometimes they are re-victimized.

3. Inability to seek help. Survivors continue to isolate themselves from others except for those who won't challenge their increasingly self-destructive behavior. They cut themselves off from those who could help by quietly withdrawing from them, being openly hostile, or by openly giving up.

4. Acting on self-destructive impulses. Feeling hopeless and without any healthy emotional support, the survivor will act on his self-destructive thinking and feelings. He may cut himself or drive too fast. The survivor may act this way to "feel *something*" if he is feeling numb and cut off from the living. Or he may do dangerous things to distract himself from feeling so out of control on the inside. He may also act self-destructively as a way to punish himself for the sins he believes he has committed.

5. Option reduction. During this phase survivors feel trapped by their pain and their inability to manage their lives. Their behavior becomes increasingly out of control so that it begins to seriously affect their health and relationships. They have overwhelming feelings of helplessness and hopelessness with an intense fear of losing everything they've worked so hard to get. There is strong fear and they feel there is no way out other than insanity, chemical use, or suicide.

6. Emotional or physical collapse. They are unable to further manage their emotions or health. Severe emotional illness such as a psychotic break or chronic panic attacks are common. Diseases occur which are often "abuse specific" such as pelvic inflammatory disease, difficult menstrual periods, or urinary tract infections. Sometimes chronic diseases which have been in remission become activated such as chronic fatigue syndrome or lupus.

7. Re-victimization and reenactments. When the survivor is trapped by poor boundaries, poor judgment, social isolation, and emotional and physical collapse, it is common that she is re-victimized. She is once again sexually abused. She is also frequently exposed to abuse reenactments wherein she is not actively re-abused but is in situations which feel to her much like the original abuse.

134

Phase IV: Deterioration

The end result of this loss of control is deterioration. The most common symptoms are:

1. Suicide or homicide attempts. The survivor makes a serious attempt on his life such as an overdose, cutting or stabbing himself, or engaging in games of Russian roulette with loaded guns or speeding cars. Sometimes survivors will make a homicide attempt, but this is rare due to the way they typically blame themselves.

2. Debilitating shame. Sexual abuse is deeply shaming. Survivors at this stage will accept the shame as inherently theirs and see no way out. The shame further strengthens their self-destructiveness or they become immobilized.

3. Abuse reenactment. They are in contact with abusive people and in situations which create for them a high potential for being re-abused.

4. Life-threatening problems. They may develop serious medical problems requiring emergency care or emotional conditions which require psychiatric hospitalization.

5. Relapse to chemical use. At this time the survivor begins using chemicals again as a way to numb her pain, provide punishment for her sense of shame, or to prove to herself that she will always be an addict.

6. Retreat into pathology. This is when the survivor has exhausted *all* her resources and requires hospitalization for a medical or psychiatric condition. To not hospitalize is inviting death through medical complications from an alcohol or drug-related accident, a disease, or a completed suicide.